Sexual Deviation:

PSYCHOANALYTIC INSIGHTS

THE RESEARCH STUDY GROUP

Participants

Mortimer Ostow, New York, Chairman
Peter Blos, New York
Sidney Furst, New York
George Gero, New York
Mark Kanzer, New York
Daniel Silverman,* Philadelphia
Richard Sterba, Detroit
Arthur Valenstein, Boston

Guests

Jacob A. Arlow, New York
Earl Loomis, New York
Ernest Rappaport, Chicago

*Dr. Silverman withdrew from the project in 1967 because of ill health. He died in 1971.

Sexual Deviation:

PSYCHOANALYTIC INSIGHTS

edited by

Mortimer Ostow, M.D.

with the assistance of
Martha H. Gillmor

Quadrangle / The New York Times Book Co.

Library of Congress Catalog Card Number:
73-79926
International Standard Book Number:
0-8129-0393-5

Design by Emily Harste
Production by Planned Production

CONTENTS

PREFACE

This is the second publication based upon the research activities of the Psychoanalytic Research and Development Fund. The first *Psychic Trauma* (edited by Sidney Furst) was based upon a research conference. This book is based upon the transactions of a research study group which met 35 times during the years 1964 through 1968. The method employed and its rationale are described below in the Introduction, and the regular participants and guests are listed opposite the title page. It is our hope that our colleagues will find this a helpful contribution to their understanding and treatment of sexual deviation.

The Psychoanalytic Research and Development Fund is a private corporation whose purpose is to conduct and sponsor research and education in psychoanalysis. Herman Nunberg was its first president. He was succeeded by Peter Neubauer, who was in turn succeeded by me, and most recently Bernard Pacella has been serving as president. Sidney Furst has been professional director of the Fund. The Fund has been supported by contributions of individuals, foundations, and corporations. We are grateful to all of these for their support and confidence.

In press now is a similarly conducted psychoanalytic study of the action of chemical agents used in psychiatric therapy. A similar project on aggression and one on child development are currently in process. We are also launching a major new endeavor on the Future of Psychoanalysis.

The material in this volume has been divided into three parts: the Introduction describes our method and its rationale; Part One presents the theoretical formulations extracted from the transcript; and Part Two presents six of the eight major case histories, much as the analysts reported them to the group. The other case histories could not be presented properly without possibly betraying the identities of the subjects. We decided to include complete protocols in order to give our colleagues the opportunity to examine the material from which the theoretical conclusions were drawn. The protocols might have been summarized in the interest of brevity, but we felt that the reader should have access to the raw data used as the springboard for discussion.

I should like to thank Martha H. Gillmor for her skillful assistance in extracting the material from the transactions and reorganizing it to create this book.

Mortimer Ostow, M.D.
Vice President
Psychoanalytic Research and
Development Fund

INTRODUCTION

The amount of generalizable information that can be obtained by the psychoanalyst from his private practice is, unavoidably, limited. The paucity of such information limits research, so that recent years have brought us few new hard facts, except for those obtained from observation of young children, and few really useful therapeutic innovations. Theoretical formulations which have been proposed offer little that is useful in the consulting room.

Let us consider the difficulties that obstruct psychoanalytic research. The individual psychoanalyst has contact with a limited number of patients in his entire professional experience, and with a relatively small number at any given time. His observations and perceptions are not consistently and routinely exchanged with his colleagues, so he lacks the opportunity to hear corroborative opinions and objective evaluations of his generalizations and hypotheses. He has access to few data derived from observation of a large number of patients.

The restricted nature of psychoanalytic practice holds the danger, for any analyst, that he will develop idiosyncratic or stereotyped interpretations of the limited volume of phenomena he encounters. Collaborative investigation as presented in this book would seem to offer maximum potential for retaining the spirit of psychoanalytic investigation and treatment, while providing a vehicle for the fruitful exchange of ideas and an accumulation—both intensive and extensive—of knowledge.

For research, if not primarily for therapeutic purposes, records of data obtained during psychoanalytic sessions should be available to the professional community. But any practicable system of record keeping should also meet the following requirements: (1) Records must be sufficiently ample to give a useful picture of what is going on but not so voluminous that they are unmanageable; (2) preparation of the records must not distract the psychoanalyst from his therapeutic work; (3) records must be so organized that the data are easily retrievable. The specific issue of record keeping was not a primary concern in this project. However, this study group was fortunate in that the participants had all maintained session-by-session clinical records of psychoanalytic transactions for a significant portion of each analysis. These records provided the data considered by the group.

The discussions that evolved from these considerations elicited areas of agreement and disagreement, a critical examination of many assumptions, and eventual consensus on several issues. Six experienced, thoughtful, and creative psychoanalysts were asked to cooperate in this group. All agreed to meet together approximately *once a month* during the academic year, for a period of four to five years, in order to present cases relevant to the chosen topic, and to study the case material with a view toward achieving new and original insights. In this way we hoped to make available to each participant the experience of the other members of the group, not merely through case presentation, but also in individual responses to the presentations. In the discussion of each extensive case presentation, the participants offered supporting or conflicting observations drawn from other cases which were often introduced in vignette form. In this way, although only eight cases were studied in detail, at least thirty or forty different cases were considered during the course of the discussions as each of the participants contributed data from his entire clinical experience.

We hoped to subject all formulations to group criticism so that useful and valid generalizations would be evaluated, weaknesses of formulations would be exposed, and the hypotheses voiced by any one of the group would be examined, modified, and extended by the others.

A primary objective was to make the formulations of the study group available to the profession. To facilitate this goal, all sessions were tape-recorded and transcripts were distributed to the participants. The transactions of each meeting were then reduced to précis form and the principal conclusions were summarized and presented at the opening of the subsequent session. These summaries were then discussed in order to correct misunderstandings, to offer the opportunity for modifications, and to establish continuity in the transactions. This publication, then, presents the major observations and formulations which were offered by members and also fragments of the discussion in which these suggestions were presented as well as the responses which they elicited.

Happily, the procedure worked well in practice. Each of the colleagues whom we approached, all busy and distinguished clinicians, was attracted to the idea and agreed to participate. Of the original participants in the study group, excluding the two members of the Psychoanalytic Research and Development Fund (Mortimer Ostow, M.D., and Sidney S. Furst, M.D.), one withdrew after four years because of illness. During the last year of discussions, additional colleagues were invited to present case material which was not available to the original group. The participating analysts were: Peter Blos, Ph.D.; George Gero, M.D.; Mark Kanzer, M.D.; Daniel Silverman, M.D.; Richard F. Sterba, M.D.; and Arthur F. Valenstein, M.D. The guests who participated for varying periods of time in the discussion group were: Jacob A. Arlow, M.D.; Robert C. Bak, M.D.; Earl A. Loomis, M.D.; and Ernest A. Rappaport, M.D.

There were thirty-five sessions; that is, about *seven meetings a year*. In view of the fact that some of the regular participants had to travel to attend the meetings and that all were heavily occupied with professional work, writing, and organizational activity, attendance was extraordinarily regular.

The group believes that the reason for this fidelity was that each participant respected the others and considered the project important. The members also developed some ties of mutual affection and regard so that each meeting became a pleasant social encounter while retaining its professional purpose. Finally, and this was perhaps most important, the group became visibly creative, and this satisfying creativity lent vitality and enthusiasm to the entire project.

When we began, each participant explained his own approach to the problem and, in the discussion, demonstrated how it applied to each case in turn. He elicited responses from the others with respect to the relevance and usefulness of his approach in each case, then modified and extended his own theory appropriately in the light of these responses. As each member of the group understood the value and usefulness of other approaches, he began to use them comfortably and to integrate the various perspectives.

This process may be illustrated by tracing the development and combination of a few of the themes which emerged in the discussion. One member was impressed by the capacity of perverse individuals for imagery, and by their unusual perceptual sensitivity. A second member of the group was particularly aware of action as a highly preferred mode of expression and behavior. Early in the project these two approaches were combined to yield the view that the perverse individual requires a degree of literalness and concreteness in his experience of object relations far beyond that required by others. A third member of the group was impressed by the observation that the perverse individual tends to identify with his object in a primitive way rather than in a manner appropriate to the pubertal youth and the adolescent. Normal identification at these ages leads to superego formation, while the identification of the perverse individual does not. This observation, combined with the previous synthesis, led to the formulation that the perverse individual tends to seek out the lost object and to identify with him via a magical merging, using perception and action in an archaic way. Perverse individuals do not relate to their objects as whole persons; they relate instead to part objects, in such a way that no introject remains to form the nucleus of an ego ideal or a superego.

Later still, another member introduced a concept that the ego of a perverse individual tolerates inconsistency and contradiction far more easily than does that of the nonperverse individual.

This idea, too, was examined and found to be generally applicable and useful. It was then related to the previous formulation in the following way: The ego of the perverse individual, instead of acquiring a superego, acquires a number of independent and frequently inconsistent identifications and identities. Any of these might be reinforced at an appropriate moment by magical perceptual incorporation. In psychoanalytic therapy, it is difficult to determine which identity is accessible to influence, since verbal communication carries very little weight with perverse individuals. This raised the question of whether some sort of literal experience should be provided for the treatment of the perverse patient.

I emphasize the evolution of concepts during the group's deliberations because it is not "visible" in the form in which they are presented in this report. Since the statements which follow were extracted from various points in the discussion and organized topically, they do not always reflect the development of ideas which resulted from the intellectual impact of the data upon the participants, nor the interaction of the members' thought processes. This evolutionary development is achieved by group process. It is true that the nucleus of each idea arises within an individual. However, the gestation of new ideas can be stimulated and encouraged if hypotheses are examined sympathetically but objectively and related to the experience and ideas of other psychoanalysts.

It is interesting to note that even individual sessions of the group displayed a concrete dynamic character. Most of the discussions were based upon recently presented case material. A few consisted of reactions to the summaries of the immediately preceding sessions. Yet in most sessions a main theme emerged and was then developed in discussion. The evolution of these themes in individual sessions, and their synthesis during the course of the project, were the expression of the creative process in which the group engaged. I believe the appreciation of the creativeness of this endeavor was the chief attraction of the project for the participants.

Several of our observations may be helpful to colleagues who wish to organize similar research groups:

The composition of the group and the careful selection of its members are crucial. The participants should be articulate individuals, old enough to have broad experience but not entrenched in rigid or inflexible positions.

In general, the busier and the more reluctant they are to undertake a new commitment, the more likely they are to become valuable contributors.

They should be congenial and they should command the respect of their colleagues.

They should all be vitally interested in fundamental psychoanalytic issues, but not irrevocably committed to a fixed point of view.

With respect to the case reports the group found that the more extensive and intensive they were, the better. Case reports that were presented over the course of five or six meetings were more productive than those which were completed in one or two. It is uncertain, however, when the effectiveness of the presentations would have reached the point of diminishing returns. Ideally, the case reports should include the presentation of large amounts of raw psychoanalytic data.

There was some question about the optimal duration of each session. Throughout this project the group met for one-and-a-half hour periods. The sessions might have been profitably extended without reaching a point of discouraging fatigue. The meetings were held *once a month* so that the project would not become too burdensome for any individual but would retain its momentum and continuity. We felt the high point of enthusiasm was reached between the fourth and fifth year, and the project was terminated at that point because we preferred to stop before the enthusiasm subsided.

What was accomplished? Obviously, no one problem concerned with sexual perversion was completely solved. No incontrovertible conclusions were established, nor were any original methods for treatment devised. However, the chief issues encountered in the treatment of perversion were examined and some novel formulations were developed. The group's discussions of the genesis and dynamics of sexual perversion and ego function in this behavior were especially productive, and the implications of the resulting formulations for the treatment process were considered. Certain areas were not adequately covered—especially perversion among female patients and children. The group felt better able to understand the phenomenon of sexual perversion at the end of the project, and to treat patients more effectively. In this book we try to convey to our colleagues what we have learned.

We recommend that others who are interested in promoting psychoanalytic research try the method which we have utilized.* We recommend also that further studies be devoted to the subject of sexual perversion both to check and extend the hypotheses which we present here, and to study those areas which we have omitted.

Mortimer Ostow
Chairman

*We have conducted similar study groups for the purpose of investigating the psychodynamics of drug therapy, the psychology of aggression, and new findings in child development, and have found the method equally applicable.

PART ONE
Argument

Chapter I
THE DEFINITION
OF PERVERSION

In the group's judgment, there was still no better definition of perverse sexuality than the one Freud provided in his "Three Essays." In that work, Freud used the term "inversion" to denote deviant behavior with respect to the *object* of the sexual instinct, and the term "perversion" to denote behavior in which there was deviation with respect to the *aim* of the sexual instinct. The distinction between inversion and perversion is not generally used; the group used the term "perversion" for both. Freud also noted that sexual behavior must be considered pathological only when the deviation was fixed and predominant.

In subscribing to this view the group seemed to be adopting norms suggested by biological—that is, reproductive—function. Yet this judgment was rooted in an aggregate of clinical experience which suggested that deviant behavior conforming to this definition was usually accompanied by other signs of mental illness, and that if these defining factors were absent, other indications of pathology did not appear nearly so consistently.

The group subscribed, too, to Freud's assertion that perverse activity became the primary means of the subject's sexual gratification. The members did not, however, believe that the occurrence of occasional normal intercourse invalidated the diagnosis of perversion. It was commonly found, for example, that among married persons with perverse sexual patterns the sexual drive found its major outlet in perverse activity with extramarital partners, even though the individual concurrently carried on what appeared to be a relatively normal—though lackluster and perfunctory—sex life within the marriage.

True perverse behavior is imperative and insistent; it is inappropriate when judged by any reality-based criteria. The need to be beaten, for example, exists in circumstances which—in the strictest reality sense—neither invite nor suggest beating as an appropriate activity. Fetishistic fixation, although it clearly possesses personal and unconscious meaning, is ordinarily incomprehensible to others.

Perverse behavior may be either ego syntonic or ego dystonic. Often, it is ego syntonic when the individual is driven by his perverse craving and ego dystonic after gratification has dissipated the need.

Should an action be labeled as perverse even if it occurs without reference to a partner? Dr. Valenstein formulated the view that clinical perversion was heavily invested with a narcissistic element and did not require the actual participation of an object. When an object was chosen, he noted, it was often selected to represent, in some manner, the subject himself. The actual or "surrogate" object—whether physically present or not—often played a strictly defined role that conformed to the subject's fantasy requirements. The *solitary* act, in these terms, was even more narcissistic in character and complied *more,* rather than less, with the clinical definition of perversion. Cases where there was no object involvement, even in representational form, suggested that no object could be imagined to satisfy the narcissistic need.

In support of this formulation Dr. Sterba observed that Freud's definition did not require that the perversion be acted out with an object. No one questioned, he noted, that solitary acts of fetishism and transvestitism were perversions. Masturbation and ritualistic behavior were both action-oriented, in contrast to pure fantasy, and in fantasy, at least, were usually object-directed as well. Dr. Furst noted that in one of his papers, Herman Nunberg observed that though the masturbation fantasy varied, the focus on the significance of the *act* was not lost. The act itself, implied Nunberg, was a manifestation of perverse behavior since its nature was bisexual: For the male, the genital was the male and the hand the female; for the female, the relationship was reversed.

Qualifying the importance of the distinction between action and fantasy, Dr. Gero proposed that the fundamental task was to elucidate why, for the perverse individual, the aim was different or remained infantile, or the object was different: "Whether the person acted, or whether it [the aim or object] merely pervaded his fantasy life, did not seem to be the essential issue."

Perhaps the role of the object was obscured. For example, a part object may have been denoted by a symbol such as a fetish, or the object absorbed into a narcissistic identification. In one example, the individual's action was limited to masturbation while gazing at his mirror image. But whether performed alone or with a partner, the behavior often involved a symbolic reenactment of some childhood experience—usually one concerned with the mother.

Clearly, then, even solitary behavior could be labeled as perverse if it was fixed and predominant in character. But should an obsession involving a perverse fantasy only be considered a perversion? Can a category of the *inhibited* perverse individual analogous to the inhibited neurotic be defined? This complex aspect of the characterization of perversion could be clarified if the operative stress were placed not so much on the *action* component as on *deviation* in aim and object. Within this broader framework, an obsessive though unimplemented fantasy of a perverse nature could be correctly considered a specific type of perversion.

The role of the genital was clearly important in defining perversion. Perverse behavior usually occurred in two distinct phases: the specific perverse activity, followed by apparently normal heterosexual intercourse in which the person's potency was augmented by the antecedent perverse behavior.

In one case studied by the group, the patient achieved potency in intercourse after he had been beaten by his wife (Case IV). In another, the subject was able to engage in normal intercourse with adequate potency only after a prostitute had urinated on him (Case I). In one dramatic example of a biphasic, mandatory sequence, a patient had to examine his partner's pharynx before intercourse could take place.

The cases considered by the group revealed that perverse behavior usually terminated with genital orgasm no matter where the stimulus was applied. Though the major source of gratification lay in the extragenital stimulation, genital orgasm seemed to constitute the "final common path" of sexual discharge. There was, however, no evidence concerning what kind of climax is achieved by perverse men who have had their external genitals removed. It is, of course, uncertain whether the sexual excitement invariably finds a genital outlet.

In our discussions, perversion and inversion—that is, homosexuality—were treated as two aspects of the same disorder, largely because they are almost always associated. However, under certain cultural conditions and when it exists without the qualities of compulsion and fixity, homosexual behavior need not necessarily be perverse.

The association of these two conditions was justified on theoretical grounds because (1) the developmental arrest required for one appeared to favor the other; (2) both phenomena represented infantile fixations, with respect to the object in homosexuality, and to the aim in perversion; (3) narcissism, infantilism, and acting-out were common to both perversion and homosexuality; and (4) homosexuality was sometimes used as a defense against other forms of sexual deviation which would become predominant in heterosexual relationships if they were permitted.

Sexual promiscuity alone was considered perverse when it clearly violated cultural attitudes, but only if it was compulsive and fixed. Promiscuity was frequently, though not always, associated with other overt perversions, especially sadism and masochism. Theoretically, compulsive promiscuity was created by the need to find a suitable object; one that could not be found in any actual, achieved relation. The search for the object in promiscuity had a defensive function, but that did not necessarily make it perverse. And though promiscuity was associated with oedipal inhibition and the need to act out preoedipal tendencies, perversion played a role in only some instances.

Similar criteria must be applied in the characterization of incest. The occasional incestuous act in cultures that do not strenuously proscribe it need not necessarily be designated a perversion. The qualities of drive, fixity, and predominance, and the overriding of cultural disapproval render the incestuous act perverse.*

Even with the application of the criteria of primacy and drive, a clear-cut diagnosis of clinical perversion may be difficult. It is possible, for example, to list a series of seemingly perverse activities ranging from least to most abnormal that could instead be classified as perverse *tendencies*:

> The persistence of pregenital components in masturbation fantasy and in normal, heterosexual intercourse;
>
> Investment of a major portion of the libidinal stream in pregenital masturbation fantasies, but without perverse action;
>
> Perverse masturbation fantasy with solitary action, such as masturbating before a mirror or masturbation with a fetish;
>
> Perverse action with a partner limited to a single discrete mode of discharge; and
>
> A variety of polymorphous perverse actions with a partner.

As Dr. Valenstein noted, there appeared to be a significant *qualitative* distinction between the persistence of pregenital tendencies expressed in masturbation fantasies—tendencies that are common if not universal—and the effectuation of the impulse through some form of action. This distinction, Dr. Blos observed, was supported by the observation that patients who engaged in perverse behavior with a partner resisted treatment more than those whose tendencies were restricted to fantasy.

The perverse action, suggested Dr. Valenstein, betrayed a "primacy" of character that ultimately interfered with genitality in heterosexual terms. The determination must ultimately be concerned with the qualitative and quantitative characteristics of clinical perversion and the nature of the (developmental) arrest involved: those sine qua non elements that contributed to a fixation which became structuralized as the main biological and functional expression of genitality.

---

*One could maintain, however, that to overcome the powerful taboo that prevails in this culture, any incestuous act would have to be driven by such a powerful impulse that the term "perversion" would necessarily apply.

The *biological* definition of perversion, largely the one accepted in our culture, utilized the reproductive function as a norm. The *clinical* definition required (1) that the primary sexual act be other than heterosexual intercourse (2) that it lead to orgastic discharge (3) that it often be performed with the aid of some apparatus; and (4) that it take as its object something representing a primary object, usually the mother. The sexual object may be some feature of the self; it may be symbolized by the apparatus; or some other person may play a carefully defined role.

Chapter II
THE ROLE OF EARLY EXPERIENCES

Two broad lines of approach were taken in the group's consideration of the etiology of perversion. As outlined by Dr. Valenstein, the first was the *developmental* approach, which viewed perversion in terms of relatively conflict-free and possibly preverbal—or at least pregenital—experience. In this experience, the individual's sexuality found points of fixation according to actual seduction and aggressivity which channelized patterns of discharge. Conceptually, this approach did not necessarily involve concern with intrapsychic conflict, although in the vital sense it did not exclude the overdetermining influence of conflict and conflict resolution upon the structuring of behavior.

The second approach emphasized the growing importance of *conflict*—in both pre-oedipal and oedipal themes. This approach, the more traditional view, had as its focal point the areas of anxiety and conflict solutions. In Dr. Valenstein's judgment, there could be no truly dynamic formulation of either the roots or dynamics of perversion unless both approaches were considered.

Although a complete understanding of

the pathogenesis of perversion could not be obtained from clinical data alone, such material provided the most fruitful source of information about its psychological components.

As a general formulation of the origin of a perversion, Dr. Ostow suggested that "anxiety in early experiences is libidinized and the traumatic situation is reenacted—with certain modifications —under conditions in which the person retains control."

The significance of constitutional and hereditary factors seemed questionable, or at the most, suggestive. Though psychoanalytic material per se could not resolve this fundamental aspect of the pathogenesis of perversion, the case material available to the group strongly favored several focal points for future analytic and experimental investigation. Two of these areas seemed likely to produce fruitful and provocative results: the special perceptual and the motoric-functional patterns in perversion. In the former, the pathology of perverse mechanisms seemed closely tied to an unusually vivid, almost eidetic quality of visual experience. The cases considered by the group also pointed to a possible hereditary predisposition, predilection, or *Anlage* for action that partly structured the discharge of aggressive and libidinal drives and impulses.

In combination with these complex and still obscure constitutional elements, the group's discussions elicited a number of basic and interrelated factors that appeared to play a role in the development and dynamics of perversion:

> modes of achieving identification, e.g., imitation as opposed to genuine adoption of ego orientation and superego values;
>
> nature of oedipal conflicts and their resolution;
>
> specific fixating traumas in childhood;
>
> body image of the self and object;
>
> anal and oral experiences in early development;
>
> adaptive success in isolating pregenital aggression;
>
> interplay between parent, child, and siblings in reinforcing proclivities toward perverse patterns of development;
>
> central differences in male and female physiology;
>
> narcissistic needs as reflections of ego weakness and id limitations; and

the action outcome required by drive discharge according to gratification patterns.

In addition to these and other etiological factors, the cases studied by the group typically furnished a spectrum of early experiences which appeared to contribute to the evolution of the adult disorder. Because such experiences were so common in cases of perversion, and since the specific perverse acts were often actual or symbolic replications of these early experiences, they appeared to play a vital role in the genesis of perversion.

In attempting to define the types of experiences that were primary etiological factors, the group often used the term "misconception" to describe the responses to such traumatic events. In this connection, Dr. Valenstein noted that:

"A central issue was whether, at least for a substantial number of clinical subjects, there was something grounded in their literal experience that organized highly idiosyncratic pathways for instinctual discharge, thus structuring deviant ways of achieving libidinal and aggressive satisfaction. The use of the term 'misconception,' in this context, must be understood in a variety of ways. There were 'misconceptions' that lacked the underscoring, the concrete crystallization, arising from a highly charged and vital experience. Or, one could speak of a 'misconception' that was actually organized around literal experience, very much as the psychotic experiences his misconstrued perceptions.

"The focus must be on what may be called 'experiential misconception.' The historical question of whether the root of neurosis lay in the literal seduction and abuse of the young child was so distressing to Freud that he was tempted to drop this line of investigation. But he then proposed that, since not every child is literally seduced and abused, the child must misconstrue, must misunderstand, and that he constructed his fantasies on the structure or the impetus of an erotic life that already existed. In ths way, the matter moved to an emphasis on misconception and fantasy.

"On this basis, we no longer need to count upon the existence of a 'real' event; the misconception *is* in fact experiential. The perverse individual's fantasy life and consequent behavior seemed, most often, centered on the way in which the body seemed to work or was experienced to work. Perhaps, phase-specific seductive maneuvers and organizing experiences could help clarify the pregenital organization of the erotic life of those who later turned to perverse behavior."

In elaborating on this issue, Dr. Furst said:

"In a sense there was a continuum with the pure misconception on one end and the actual experience on the other. In our clinical work we can sometimes see how the process starts with a misconception and takes a form in which it is supported by some aspects of reality. It need not be completely substantiated; various circumstantial observations may tend to support it. As the 'misconception' takes shape, it may change to conform with those elements in reality that more effectively give it substance.

"In one example, a patient who was frequently given enemas by his mother became quite excited at an early age on noticing that an enema bag in the bathroom had two tips—a large and a small one. He began to masturbate anally and it was only with great difficulty—since he subscribed to the cloacal theory and was not aware of a female organ—that he progressed to phallic masturbation. Here, his fixation on an anal level, starting from that initial observation and experience, gradually became reinforced and altered its shape to conform to supporting elements in the environment."

An issue that underlay any consideration of the dynamic character of traumatic "misconceptions" was whether the channeling of behavior in perversion—particularly in the perverse ritual—was invariably based on *specific* infantile events. Since the material critical to such a judgment was often unavailable to the analyst, a hypothesis would be that the "structural" elements were invariably present even though there was not a precise replication of the formative experience.

Several of the discussants asserted that a clear and behaviorally precise replication was involved in every ritualistic perverse act.

Dr. Valenstein's position was that: "A perversion always has its infantile representations and its paradigm. The nature of the perverse act has a prototype in literal experience somewhere in childhood—even if we never find it. It may be buried in amnesia or concealed in some manner, but it is there somewhere."

Though not presented in full, a case mentioned during the study group's meetings provided striking documentation for this view. The decisive trauma, for this patient, occurred when the patient was about two-and-a-half years old. Although completely submerged by amnesia, a seduction by an older sister was confirmed when parts of the various rituals were reconstructed in analysis. Most important, the original experience contained the same verbal elements that returned compulsively in the perverse ritual.

A configuration of early childhood experiences also indicated how a combination of generalized factors and specific incidents could provide the elements for a particular action pattern in the adult. In one example of solitary perverse behavior, the patient used handcuffs on himself or bound his scrotum with a cord which was thrown over a chandelier and tied to his wrists which were tied behind his back. During analysis, the patient recalled three events which seemed to have formative significance for the solitary perversion:

1. Occasional loss of bowel control as a child, during which the scrotum—though not the penis—was covered with the stool, thus providing a focus of concern;

2. A memory of his mother's having used a nighttime "peter bag"—a rubber urine receptacle—which was tied onto his penis during a period of enuresis in his fifth or sixth year; and

3. Recollection of a violently unpleasant sensation produced by the "strangling" embrace of a grandmother. The patient "couldn't stand" to be embraced by his wife, and had to extricate himself on such occasions.

Early roots of an ultimate structuring of behavior were also seen in a patient's primary masturbation fantasy of being tied down by women. This patient occasionally tied his penis with rubber bands before intercourse. For many months during childhood, his hands had been tied to the crib to prevent thumb sucking.

Another case (Case I) demonstrated how a combination of experiences and supporting factors in the environment converged about a central, initial misconception to structure both the ultimate form of perverse behavior and a "preferred" fixation to which the individual regressed. In this case, although the patient often watched his mother dress and undress, he was not aware that she had a vagina. He believed that her anus was the only opening in the lower part of her body. His mother was a rather overdemanding, obsessive woman who imposed strict toilet training on the patient. The patient—who asked prostitutes to undress standing above him so that he could press his face into their perinea—kept a list of his perineal contacts, much as a schedule of bowel movements might be kept by a mother. In commenting on this case, Dr. Valenstein observed that there seemed to be "an enormous pregenital fixation with instinctual interests from the earliest period in life, overdetermined by an insistent, intransigent mother. This libidinal fixation, responsive to the mother's orientation, became colored by anal and urinary qualities."

A related issue was the dynamic character of the patient's regression to a preferred fixation in response to frustration. Dr. Ostow observed that "if the frustration is internally generated usually an organic connection exists between the inhibition on the one hand, and the fixation point to which the individual regressed on the other. These phenomena are not unrelated; the point of fixation to which the person regresses appears in the fantasy which records the threat from which he retreats."

In support of this observation, a member introduced an example in which a patient fantasized that when a woman urinates she "creates" a penis which becomes "erect." This patient recalled several events related to female urination:

> frequent sensory impressions in women's toilets to which he had been taken by his mother;
> a maid who made a "sound of mighty water" when urinating while standing, and who was wearing a long dress which hid her body.

The patient—who as a child often urinated in public places as an adult urinated in the bathtub, in the sink, or from the window of his apartment. He often finds himself standing near the ladies' lounge at a favorite theatre, directing women to the toilet. He has dreams of suffocating in tunnel streams into which he has been "flushed."

Dr. Ostow commented that "the fantasy involved the woman's

creation of a penis through urination, and the man's ability to kill a woman by urinating into her. One of his efforts to deal with castration anxiety and castration horror was to regress to phallic urinary fantasies in which the urinary *function* becomes the real penis in place of an actual anatomic penis. By this token, the fact that the woman's urinary stream seemed more vigorous and larger meant that she really had a penis and that it was larger than the man's." As an adult, he continued to respond to the threat of the female genital by reviving, in his actions, his childhood fantasy that to urinate meant to possess a penis.

Among the cases studied, particularly cases of homosexuality, the attitudes and behavior of the mother appeared to contribute an essential element to the development of the individual's predilection for unusual forms of sexual gratification. In most of the instances of male homosexuality, as with male perversion in general, manifestations of castration anxiety and phallic narcissism were common. This strong fixation on the male organ and a phobic aversion to the female genital were frequently related to the earliest childhood impressions of parents.

One case discussed by the group emphatically suggested the fundamental importance of "castration shock" in the development of patterns of gratification and sexuality. Here (Case I), the patient vividly described a childhood bathroom incident, in which he saw a female cousin's nude body. To his horror, he found that there was no penis, but an "awful, red, gaping wound." The patient in this case was a voyeur and, driven by enormous aggressivity and rage, had fantasies of ripping open the female genital to find the penis that must be hidden within.

In most of such cases, the mother was unusually hostile and aggressive, often also forcing seductive play and display. In many instances, she troubled the child by alternating seduction and frustration. In some such cases, Dr. Furst claimed, the child may have erotized and found virtue in the frightening seduction experience. He became fixated, and wished to renew this experience of being overwhelmed by the mother. It was not simply that he was aware of being unable to control the mother, but that he longed to be overwhelmed by her, although the prospect was terrifying.

Overall, a complex interplay of maternal assertiveness (frequently in contrast to the father's passivity), aggressive demands, seductiveness, and frustration made the female role seem to the child dramatically more desirable than the male. A similar developmental influence could be exerted by an excessively demanding mother through humiliation, unreasonably stringent task setting, and frequent reminders of failure. By her constant demonstration of his inability to live up to her expectations, the mother disparaged the effectiveness and value of the young boy's sexual identity—his penis.

One patient felt that his mother made such impossible demands on him and was a continuing source of humiliation. His mother clearly humiliated him; in effect, she said, "You're castrated," and at the same time said, "You must accomplish; you must be successful." His mother defined the problem for him and said, "Here's how you've got to go about solving it: You've got to get yourself a penis somewhere, because you don't have one of your own." As a result, he said, "I'll get it the way my father got his."

In his own marriage, he recapitulated the same problem with the phallus that he had with his mother. His mother said, "You've got to get one somewhere" and in a sense his wife pushed him in the same direction with her frigidity. He interpreted that to mean, "You are no good, because you're castrated, and you've got to do something if you want me to love you; you've got to get yourself a phallus as big as your father's." So she pushed him into various types of homosexual expression just as, in a certain sense, his mother had done.

The mother's tendency to humiliate and to set requirements that the boy could not successfully meet was sometimes mixed with overprotectiveness and, occasionally, an explicit preference for the boy to behave and even dress in a female manner.

Combinations of several basic etiological elements were present in the early childhood experiences of virtually all of the cases of male perversion studied by the group. In imitation of the mother's aggressivity, the son frequently developed a tendency toward vigorous and "excessive" *action* as a generalized mode of dealing with reality and intrapsychic conflicts.

In addition to possible genetic predisposition, what role did the mother and other figures important in early development play in ego development?

One patient alternated between aggressive heterosexual fantasies with violent outbursts toward his wife, and passive invitations to homosexual seduction. His earlier history—dominated by a demanding, phallic, and extremely active mother—displayed frequent episodes of hyperactivity, exhibitionism, and aggressiveness.

In heuristic theory, it was suggested that an action-oriented mother might enhance, inhibit, or in some sense underscore her son's action system as it unfolds. In this case, the mother's role as an active, phallic, doing woman appeared to have been highly significant in the development of the patient's action system—particularly, his problems of aggression; his exhibitionistic, mischievous behavior; and his head banging, and enuresis, and urinating behind furniture. He grew up identifying with his mother's active style and also feeling the target of it. This style determined his inclination to be both the aggressor in identification, and the passive victim who flees into inhibition. He appeared to have experienced a honeymoon phase with his mother, which connected with his deeply rooted feeling that coitus is filthy, vile, and evil, that a quality of badness characterizes instinctual life in general. This feeling related in turn to his early "dirty" phase in anal-phallic development, and to his still earlier oral-anal sadistic phase with its head banging.

With regard to the mother's role as the "action model"—that is, interpretation of the patient's acting-out as identification with such a figure in the past—Dr. Gero commented: "The relationship would have to be more concrete. The patient's acting-out might have been causally related to acting-out which he experienced in the past. If the actor was a seducer, the seduction represented a traumatic experience, and the subject's later acting-out could result from his identification with his aggressor. But in some cases of acting-out there is nothing manifest in the past history."

In some instances, the child learned to exploit the mother's hostility as a vehicle for masochistic gratification. In others, the response took the form of a retribution drama by degrading and soiling the object. In some instances, the child found a degree of defense against her unremitting aggression and hostility by adopting an attitude of inhibition and passivity. In one such case presented to the group, this attitude served not only to blunt the mother's aggression but, in later years, provided vengeful gratification as the patient failed in many areas of endeavor.

Premature, intense, and frequent arousal by the mother may, as illustrated by a number of patients in the group, fix the child's sexual desires and fantasies to her permanently. In some cases, the mother often and flagrantly displayed her naked body to her son, who frequently felt overwhelmed and frightened. One way the son dealt with this bewildering and threatening seductiveness was to identify with the mother—in much the same way some concentration camp prisoners identified with their aggressors in an effort to adapt.

In situations of overprotectiveness, the mother may tend to frustrate the maturation of her child's motor skills, and the child may respond with intense aggressiveness. The mother's excessive affection, when followed by such frustration, may well become virtually intolerable for the child. When, in addition, he is subjected to constant ridicule and insistent demands which he cannot meet, the phallic self-esteem of the son becomes fundamentally impaired.

The origin of one boy's homosexual preferences was clearly exhibited in one vignette reported. He responded to his mother's wish that he pretend to be a girl by adopting her concern with his appearance and by comforting himself in her absence by wearing her clothing. Though in such instances the mother usually demands that the child become more feminine, at other times she might require him to conceal feminine interests by presenting a conventionally boyish appearance and manner. The mother may attempt to lend verisimilitude to her own fantasy of a little girl with a penis by demanding feminity of her son.

The role of gender identification and its relationship to body- and self-image were also considered determining elements in the ultimate action pattern of perverse behavior. Dr. Blos noted, in this connection, that a fixation on the cloaca serves as an effective elimination of gender differences, providing an uncertain self-image through "asexual compromise" that makes either identification possible.

As Dr. Valenstein observed, the quality of childhood fantasy play with respect to body image must be fundamentally affected if the fantasy was overdetermined by a "reality" resulting from reinforcement by the parent. A research project undertaken at Johns

Hopkins University related to this observation. In that study, children who had indefinite external genitalia and who had been assigned a specific gender role assumed the assigned role even though subsequent evidence determined a different anatomical character. The children in the series frequently developed secondary sex characteristics—including breasts in the case of boys—concomitant with their assigned roles.*

Dr. Valenstein made the speculative suggestion that the assumption of a specific gender role early in development may conceivably have an impact on ultimate neuro-humoral and physiological development. The body would, in effect, "follow" the direction of psychic adaptation; i.e., somatic compliance.

In reconstructing developmental factors in the individual case, or in extrapolating broader etiological patterns, it was acknowledged that many clearly formative experiences of gender identification occurred too early for precise recapture by the memory. One must be content with the dynamic evidence of these dim and distorted images as well as other classic types of psychoanalytic information. Such evidence suggests that to the child whose mother was actively hostile or even sadistic, she seemed literally to bear a penis. The indication, paradoxically, was that the image of the "castrated" woman was the most frightening of such phenomena. The threat represented by the "castrated" female genitalia was often heavily augmented by a projection of the child's own vengeful fury.

By supplying a penis for this awesome image, the child is able to dilute its fearful aspect and tame it. In a subsequent stage of defense, the mother is deprived of all sexuality and converted into a madonna figure. The male homosexual fails to progress beyond the initial defensive phase; for him, all women remain phallic and, since the woman seems more powerful than the man, he identifies with her. The male homosexual, as a result, cannot tolerate an object without a penis, and insists upon a phallic object whether or not it is associated with other aspects of femininity.

The role of the father—particularly the absence of an effectual father—often seems to provide an important element in the patho-

*See John Money, "Cytogenic and Psychosexual Incongruities with a Note on Space-Form Blindness," *American Journal of Psychiatry,* vol. 119, no. 9, pp. 820-827, March 1963.

genesis of male homosexuality. In a number of cases, the boy has been seduced by the father or older male relative. Seduction may have consisted merely of the older male's permitting excessively intimate exposure, such as sharing toilet experiences; or the seduction may have involved actual physical stimulation by the father or another male. In such instances, full masculine genital identification with the father fails to develop. Instead, the boy is arrested at the earlier developmental stage of imitative identification with the father, or at the phase of object relation. In the first case, the boy presents a conventional masculine appearance and exaggerated phallic function, but is unable to perform at the genital level. In the latter instance, he often identifies with the mother as the female lover of the father.

There was ample indication that, given an "absent" father and a dominant mother, the boy will usually have difficulty resolving the Oedipus conflict and will regress to the femininity which has received approbation from the mother. In some instances, however, homosexuality appears to be assumed partially to punish a mother who expects her son to behave conventionally in every sense although he must demonstrate an extravagant "attachment" to her.

The "classic" pattern of the male homosexual who requires a phallic object underlines the different character of childhood experiences in development of male and female perversion. The fact that members of the group had only rare occasion to consider cases of female perversion suggests that perversion may occur less frequently among females than males. It may also indicate that women with perversion patterns are less apt to come for therapeutic assistance than men. In any event, to achieve mature heterosexuality, the male must fully advance from his pregenital needs for the mother so that they will not too literally structure the character of his relationship with his marital partner.

In normal development, the male succeeds in isolating these two areas of sexual experience from each other, but in perversion he symbolically attempts to substitute the infantile for the adult relationship. The female, however, whose adult object is a different sex from her initial object, does not share the difficulty nor the dynamics of maintaining a sharp distinction between two forms of heterosexuality and two heterosexual objects; her pregenital and infantile attachment to the mother need not be so rigorously repressed. Unlike the male, whose infantile and adult "partners" are both women, she has less tendency to impose the pattern of her infantile relation onto her marital relationship in order to retain a fragment of the earliest association with the mother. For the woman, adult sexuality does not require drastic repression of infantile sexuality.

Another aspect of this asymmetry of the developmental tasks of male and female is that male and female tend to identify with the first love object, the mother, in earliest infancy. In her own experience of intercourse, the adult female can indulge a persisting infantile tendency to identify with the "discomfort" of the primal-scene mother. The same wish, in the man, would lead to castration anxiety and engender a perverse variant of his image of the primal scene: homosexual masochism or brutal sadism.

A fundamental issue which the group explored was the erotic component in the pathogenesis and patterns of perversion. They examined both the character of the literal erotic sensation brought about by the perverse act and the etiological roots of the patterns of perverse acts, including the meaning underlying their expression.

There was general agreement that masochistic acts are not simply manifestations of the aggressive drive; even the term *moral* masochism suggests a libidinal function. Sadomasochistic impulses might represent critical distortion of the *fusion* of normal aggressive and libidinal impulses toward the same object. This concept of the fusion of genitality with aggression explains how genitality can be articulated with socialized or adaptive aggression in the service of a libidinal end; gross destructiveness, subsumed under a neurotic goal, imparted a vital though abnormal continuity and force that enabled the patient to achieve sexual gratification.

On one level, the masochistic experience was viewed as a repetition compulsion with two contradictory objectives: overcoming and mastering a sadistic attack while, at the same time, submitting to it. On another level, the act of submission can be interpreted as an expiating gesture which atones for sadistic impulses toward the parent.

Dr. Ostow suggested that another mechanism may be the need for a specific pattern of action that enables the child to overcome a normal ambivalence toward his parents. This device rewards the child for deflecting the outward-directed hostility back upon himself by endowing the deflected aggression with the capacity to elicit erotic pleasure.

The group members agreed that when the young child becomes angry with the mother, and then turns the anger back upon himself, the self-direction of the aggression attracts an erotic cathexis and becomes a sexual perversion.

This theory distinguishes between the normal fusion of aggression with a libidinal element and the abnormal pattern that takes the form of a perversion. Behavior that may have commenced exclusively as an angry attack against the mother without a direct sexual aim gains a libidinal aspect and a perverse character when turned against the self and compulsively repeated.

In her conscious fantasy, one patient maintained as an adult the role of a superior and more admirable woman vis-à-vis her mother that she played for her father as a child. In her dream life, particularly in one repetitive dream with a strong erotic element, some impossible task was set for her. As she tried progressively harder with an increasing sense of degradation to meet the demand —here illustrating the fusion of the turned-about masochistic and libidinal qualities—she ultimately experienced orgasm. In fact, the patient could achieve orgasm only as a result of this repetitive dream. She found that her hostility toward her mother was both "betrayed" and partially expressed through her degradation of the mother and her oedipal seduction of the father. She resolved the hostility by turning it against herself and experiencing sexual gratification only by entertaining the fantasy of identifying with her mother in degradation.

Another case history concerned a woman who was frigid and enjoyed a masturbatory life which was explicitly sadomasochistic. Her fantasies invariably involved her brutalization; the requirement that she be humiliated was always present. The mother, who frequently indulged in shrill, shrieking outbursts against the father, had made it clear that to be a female was to be degraded, that to be a woman was a "dirty, rotten business." These two basic elements— the violent marital model and the sense of female degradation—were joined, four years later, after the arrival of a brother whom the patient "hated" and who became the object of sadistic play (which may have provided a satisfying erotic component as well as a vehicle for aggressive drives). A fourth critical factor was the fantasy, based on early play with the father, that the penis was very large, truly gigantic. In adult life, the experience of intercourse never fulfilled the expectations engendered by the patient's fantasies about the male organ.

Here, the group saw a sadomasochistic configuration of elements, in which the aggressive and erotic components were not completely "fused"; that is, they did not attenuate each other. Though the individual's development had been arrested at a certain stage through a combination of fundamental misconceptions and actual experience, the aggression remained *commingled*, rather than fused, with the eroticism.

A complex aspect of pathogenesis in perversion was illustrated in another case vignette reported to the group. The patient who occasionally beat his wife, had experienced enormous infantile anger with his mother as a result of excessive stimulation through exposure to her nude body, and frustration by her refusal to comfort him or to allow him to touch her. He responded to this frustration with sullen withdrawal. This patient imagined, while masturbating, that he was being whipped and beaten by women. Since he had never actually been beaten by his mother as a child, the form of the perversion did not precisely recreate the infantile experience. As Freud observed in his patients, beating fantasies are found in persons who have not been physically abused as well in those who have. Therefore, the masturbation fantasies in this case seemed to have originated in hostility toward the mother, which may not have initially been erotically charged, but which now shaped the image of the erotic experience.

The beating fantasy may also have served in addition to accommodate two identity strivings: on one hand, with the mother who was cold and unapproachable and whom he was punishing for frustrating him; on the other, with the castrated mother who was "beaten" in bed by the father, with whom the male child also identified. In this sense, most males with beating fantasies are likely to maintain an identification with a castrated mother, and this identification may obscure identification with—and a vengeful fury toward—the phallic mother. The accommodation becomes, then, a solution of the Oedipus complex in negative terms.

Chapter III
THE DYNAMICS OF PERVERSION

In many instances, perversion serves as a defense against anxiety—primarily, castration anxiety. The basic sources of anxiety fall into four classic patterns: (1) the very young boy is appalled by exposure to the female genital; (2) he fears castration by the father; that is, the oedipal guilt generates a fear of being punished for "intimacy" with the mother; (3) he feels helplessly impotent; and (4) he is frightened by becoming aware of sadistic impulses toward his mother. Castration anxiety may also be elicited by the drive to identify with the mother; this drive is facilitated by a strong constitutional predisposition to bisexuality.

In perversion, attempts to assuage castration anxiety involve the person's performing an act that enables him symbolically to obtain his father's penis, reassure himself of the integrity of his own penis, capture his father's love, or play the mother in relationship to a "boy" representing himself. However, a perverse act per se does not always initially control or alleviate anxiety. It may instead induce further anxiety, i.e., superego anxiety, as well as danger from without (reality). A particular act of perversion may fail to be consummated on its own terms, so that the resulting frustration not only fails to alleviate the original anxiety but elicits shame and guilt as well. One clear-cut example of this process was a case presented to the group in which the patient's perverse activity—a need to be humiliated by prostitutes in a specific fashion—helped to alleviate an enormous fear of castration. When this anxiety—which had previously existed only in relation to his wife and with other idealized women—"leaked" over into his relationships with prostitutes, the patient withdrew from his perverse "game," which no longer effectively served its purpose (Case I).

Even if it is successful in reducing anxiety, the perverse act may generate guilt, leaving the patient more unhappy than he was previously. This reaction was evident in patients who came into analysis on finding, for example, that they could not resist engaging in homosexual activities, in perverse behavior with prostitutes, or who were frightened by the "sudden" development of perverse impulses. Individuals who are predisposed to conflict and for whom the perversion is ego dystonic are most likely to be troubled by such concerns.

The person indulges in perverse heterosexual acts in the hope of proving sexual mastery, only to find that he is so overwhelmed by his partner that the anxiety is increased rather than alleviated.

The exacerbation of anxiety in a situation over which the perverse individual does not exert full control—the need to be the prime "actor" in the perverse experience—was illustrated in a number of cases presented to the group. These episodes also illuminated the complex characteristics of the chosen act itself—characteristics essential for the act to function effectively as a defense against anxiety and as a source of gratification.

In one case, a patient's experience with a prostitute suddenly became laden with anxiety when he was "hooked" into paying a larger fee than he had anticipated. For this patient, a vital element of control was his fixing a fee with the prostitute; when that expression of being in control lost its symbolic effectiveness, the event became instead a source of anxiety.

In another case, a patient with strong voyeuristic tendencies achieved gratification by attending ballet performances where he concentrated on the male dancers. But he once reported, after attending a dramatic play, that he had been "flooded" with anxiety during the performance and had been able to control the impulses aroused only by symptomatically invoking depersonalization, which was his characteristic defense against anxiety. The group hypothesized that this patient had probably been affected by a primal-scene experience, although he never reported one in the course of the analysis. The group's inference was drawn from the clinical picture, which resembled many in their experience in which primal-scene anxiety played a precipitating role in the perverse behavior. The patient's description of his anxiety reaction and the defense against it suggested that the anxiety arose either from the display of uncontrolled and unpredictable behavior, or because his perverse impulse threatened to escape from control. In other voyeuristic situations over which he exerted control—and thus minimized anxiety—the patient was able to enjoy the gratification he obtained indirectly.

In a third instance, the patient had engaged the services of a prostitute to provide the humiliating and degrading elements necessary for his specific perverse reenactment. When the prostitute became "overenthusiastic' in her role, the patient stopped the proceedings and said, "Just a minute—who's paying who? Who's in charge of this thing? You're going too far—and I'm running this show, not you!" (Case I).

Faced with such sources of residual and even augmented anxiety, the individual may attempt to restrict his gratification to fantasy, or he may depersonalize. In adopting that device, the patient finds himself split during the act of perversion; he is both participant and observer. One part of the ego is engaged in and by the act, while another part remains aloof and functions as the observer of the other self. For certain patients, such experiences of mental diplopia appear to provide a special reward. By the split, the perverse individual can convert a two-party situation into a three-party "drama"—thus reproducing the primal scene.

Dr. Arlow elaborated on this mechanism with reference to a patient who responded to a primal-scene experience with such a double identification: The patient's reaction at that time was depersonalization, which had to do with the conflict between the wish to be a participant—while actually being only an observer, and the wish to get revenge on the parents by reversing the situation—by creating situations in which the patient would be caught doing something wrong by one or the other parent.

This mechanism of depersonalization, Dr. Valenstein pointed out, often accompanies perversion. Sometimes it is formalized in a well-recognized variation: the use of a mirror during intercourse. Many people do this without recognizing it as anything more than an enrichment of sexual possibility. He mentioned that a patient and his wife who used a mirror during intercourse were like children watching. Their theme was, "This is not me." There was an interesting inhibition in full participation in that the man was split, not knowing where he should lodge his erotic satisfaction. "He could finally be more aggressive only when he looked at himself in the mirror, that is, saw himself first as the person looking at the scene in the mirror."

Depersonalization, albeit a defensive maneuver, may also give rise to separation anxiety when, for example, it is elicited in order to defend against some quasi-object relation which the perverse experience might establish.

Characteristically, the anxiety which arises from the practice of the perversion is libidinized, and thereby contributes to the sadomasochistic excitement and gratification. In this sense, the anxiety usually overdetermines the pleasure; and this libidinization makes it possible for potentially dangerous behavior to override self-preservative tendencies. Of course, libidinization of anxiety is not unique to perversion; it also occurs in counterphobic acts and in forms of dangerous behavior that are sometimes seen in individuals struggling with depression.

A critical question in the dynamics of perversion is how anxiety is sometimes resolved through nonperverse symptom formation; yet in other cases—or in the same individual, at other times—the subject responds with a perversion that constitutes the major symptomatic act defending against the anxiety.

As formulated by Dr. Ostow, the ultimate mechanism of perversion "seems to depend on how an anxiety-provoking experience is transformed into an activity that generates sexual pleasure. There must be some process by which the child's anger, and his wish to retaliate that is induced by an overwhelming experience or series of experiences, becomes—through an active or passive repetition of the actual experience or a modified version of the experience—a sexually exciting rather than a frightening event."

Focus on experience and action, relative weakness of the superego, and unresponsiveness to words or abstract concepts, are all indicators of the fixation characteristic of perversion. They represent, as expressed by Dr. Ostow, "a relative fixation at an early stage—when only action and experience had significance. This fixation occurred at a level before the superego had become effective; at a point before words had become dominant and provided a 'substitute reality' within which the individual could plan, conjecture, and solve problems."

If one views perversion, Dr. Arlow observed, as a regressive utilization of earlier forms of sexual gratification, and as their integration into a series of defensive structures organized by the ego, it becomes possible to understand how perversion and symptom formation may exist side by side. Perhaps the dichotomy should not be seen only as between symptom formation and perversion, but also as between symptom formation and character structure. "The same type of unconscious instinctual conflict, in one person," he said, "may eventuate in certain stable and persistent defensive structures leading to character formation, while in another, it leads to symptom formation."

In one sense, the essential distinction between the perverse and the neurotic method of controlling an unconscious impulse, is that the neurotic develops a neurotic symptom while the perverse subject does not. The perverse experience appears to be much more closely related to the psychotic's mode of symptom formation. More precisely, for the neurotic the symptom per se is ego alien; perversion is ego syntonic. When a perversion is not ego syntonic but continues to be practiced, it can be viewed as a neurotic compulsion superimposed upon a perversion.

This distinction, as further extended by Dr. Ostow, relates to the fact that in the case of a neurotic symptom—a hysterical paralysis or a phobic aversion, for example—the focus of the symptom is an *inhibition* of the impulse against which the individual is struggling. In perversion, however, the libido is directed toward obtaining gratification. Here, a resolution is sought essentially in terms of action and activity, or perhaps a fantasy of action—either positive or negative. The three fundamental differences, as proposed by Dr. Ostow, are:

1. Perversion is a repetitive reliving of the transformed expression of an infantile experience, while the neurotic symptom is a symbolic compromise expression of conflict among id, ego, and superego forces;

2. Superego forces are more evident in the neurotic symptom than in the perversion itself; and

3. The perverse subject, having a low tolerance for frustration and likely to be impulse-ridden, cannot use ideas and language for conflict resolution as effectively as the neurotic.

The theory that a perverse act may represent a form of rebirth experience was strongly supported in the group's examination of several cases. In Case IV, a man in his fifties—whose wife was unable to conceive—suddenly developed a need to be beaten. Though the members' interpretations of the case dynamics varied, it seemed generally clear that the perversion was utilized, through identification with the castrated woman, to reinforce symbolically an early feminine self-image as a defense against overt homosexuality. The perversion—which did not involve the genitals in the initial act—also played a role in the larger female identification process. It induced a sense of rebirth which centered about a heightened awareness of the meaning of Holy Week. In the wish for rebirth, the group saw a connection between perversion and psychosis. In both, separation anxiety generated by a disengagement from unsatisfactory object relations or some aspect of reality appeared to activate a wish for rebirth.

In perversion, withdrawal is often utilized as a mode of dealing with a variety of anxieties, such as those induced by family or vocational pressures. For those in analysis, the content and context of the analytic relationship can also create a continuously high level of anxiety. In response to such pressures, the patient may plan some sort of disengagement—often a vacation, perhaps a temporary or permanent termination of the analysis. The trend to disengagement is often heightened by the prospect of the freedom to resume or intensify perverse activities without the surveillance and potential criticism of the spouse or the analyst. But the loneliness produced by the disengagement, the fact that giving up the object is in a sense a withdrawal from reality, may in some instances precipitate the wish for rebirth similar to that found so frequently in schizophrenia.

In summary, the relation between perversion and anxiety is complex: Each act of perversion is primarily an attempt to defend against castration anxiety. The defense provided by the perversion may fail or itself become a source of anxiety, and defenses invoked against this latter anxiety may be equally ineffective. Throughout, a characteristic development is that the anxiety becomes libidinized. In terms of the "action economics" of perverse behavior, an optimal perversion is one that provides maximal gratification with minimal anxiety.

Among the clinical phenomena commonly encountered in male homosexuals are castration anxiety, phallic narcissism, aggressiveness, a heightened visual sensitivity, and early awareness of homosexual preference. Case V provided an unusually comprehensive set of clinical indicators. The patient was a young man who, as a boy, had often applied makeup and spent hours at a mirror. His homosexual experiences had begun at age fifteen, and were reinforced at eighteen when he was seduced by a schoolmaster. Deeply passive, he was repelled by young women and had no ongoing friendships. The analysis provided his only current object relation.

Among the clinical indications presented by the patient in this particular case were:

1. early feminine identification as demonstrated by transvestism in childhood, and narcissistic admiration of the mirror image;

2. horror of the female genital and denial of castration;

3. avoidance of girls and rejection of masculine activity;

4. preoccupation with fantasy life;

5. general inhibition of action;

6. self-indulgence with respect to food, clothing and possessions; and

7. a repression of hostility, with its projection onto the image of the genital.

As amply illustrated by the case material examined by the

group, the male homosexual maintains a self-image which is fixed in its infantile form; it fails to mature along with his chronological development. Specifically, he often maintains the idea that he still has the small penis that he had when a child.

A case vignette presented to the group illustrated this search for the lost or inadequate penis. The patient, whose characteristic action orientation had served him well in reality in his profession, was a married homosexual. The analyst felt that he married in order to get a mother; rather than being bisexual, he was pseudoheterosexual.

The patient told the analyst that he collected phalluses: the larger and thicker, the better. He collected phalluses not only in terms of compulsive pederastic activity, but also in the process of visualization. He claimed to be able to remember every penis he had ever seen. For him, the pain of being penetrated anally by a particularly large penis created a positive ecstasy.

He was able to function sexually with his wife by imagining, during intercourse, the most recent or most ecstatic pederastic experience he had had. Without this fantasy, he was unable to reach orgasm. Unlike many perverse individuals who use the perversion to achieve heterosexual intercourse as an end-product, this man had to search out the pederastic experience immediately after the heterosexual act.

Dr. Furst suggested that the man felt he lost his penis during heterosexual intercourse and then was impelled to find one. But Dr. Valenstein hypothesized that the patient was convinced that he had no penis at all, and this conviction reinforced the drive to collect the ideal penis.

There appears to be a variety of possible reasons for the fixation on the lost or inadequate penis. They include: memories of childhood ineffectuality in the face of a demanding but often seductive mother that persist into adult life; the young boy's masochistic desire to be overwhelmed by the dominant and sexually threatening mother; unmanageable anxieties based on early experiences of erotic stimulation by the mother and leading to a "repudiation" of the penis; and, a self-image with a small penis, retained as "protection" against the father's retribution.

The homosexual man faced with the challenge of heterosexual

intercourse will attempt to reinforce his potency through the less threatening choice of homosexual experience, enhancing his fantasies of rugged virility through gazing at his own mirror image or at the penis of a homosexual partner.

The ability to "incorporate" the desirable penis through visual stimulation indicates the multileveled character of perverse behavior. It involves—in a simultaneous and interrelated manner—a hypersensitivity of perception; a compelling predilection to fantasy; a need for concreteness and literalness of experience; the relation to body parts rather than to objects; and, overall, an action-discharge pattern that may be partially structured on the basis of constitutional elements.

Since his initial experience with the female, that is, his mother, has so often been an amalgam of seduction, frustration, and "impotence," the male homosexual is violently hostile toward women. As an adult, this hostility is primarily expressed in phallic fantasies or activity. The aggressive component in his behavior serves as one method of compensation for his "small" penis and impotent self-image.

Material reported by one member of the group indicated how a male homosexual had demonstrated his anger and aggressiveness during childhood in a number of ways. His mother was an enormously intelligent, articulate, demanding woman who had, on occasion, been explicitly seductive. Not only was the patient enuretic, but he would deliberately urinate on the floor and out the window. He was mischievous and pugnacious and, when older, took up wrestling as his favorite sport. His tantrum behavior persisted in his marital relation, and the hostility ultimately took a phallic form in a series of fantasies involving violent, sadistic sexual attacks upon his wife.

"In the whole genetic picture of this case," observed Dr. Blos, one could actually follow the vicissitudes of the aggressive drive.

> This man was given to head banging and tantrums when he was a child and, as an adult, he had a tantrum when he had intercourse. This meant that intercourse had become an uncontrollable, aggressive act. Then he turned to a controlled form of aggression— wrestling, where there's a great deal of enjoyment in a legitimate form of aggression. His turning *to* a homosexual act occurred after

he had reached the limits of his endurance with his wife in terms of rejection, whereupon he threw a tantrum, marched out of the house, wanted to retaliate. It was my impression that he *turned away* from the woman—which meant that he was *not* going to have an affair or go to a prostitute. But his aggression against the woman was so enormous that he turned to a homosexual episode as a *protective, defensive device: not to lose his control in the heterosexual act,* which he now made a battle. He was really so much at the mercy of his primitive aggression that he had to turn away from that form of gratification, which was far more ego syntonic.

In light of his unmitigated aggression, it seemed that there was almost a drive defusion—that his aggressive impulse had become so primitive and violent that the homosexual act was the defensive procedure he adopted in order not to destroy.

The tendency of the perverse subject to relate to part rather than to whole objects appeared to nurture the persistence of primitive aggressiveness. The patient of one member of the study group—a young, latent homosexual male—developed an enormous amount of aggression in response to a mother who made stringent demands but who "never gave him anything." The aggression became intertwined with his phallic strivings, and his fantasies of intercourse involved imagery of massive violence and destruction: the penis penetrating up through the woman's body and out through the head, destroying everything in its path. A related instance of phallic sadism was illustrated in another case of a patient who experienced the heterosexual orgasm as a violent, explosive act. He could keep from "injuring" his partner only by becoming impotent—suggesting that in perversion the fused libidinal and aggressive drives are sometimes wrenched apart.

It is interesting to note, however, that the homosexual's impotence, which functions to "protect" the female partner against his sadistic attack, also injures her by depriving her of sexual gratification. In this way, the repressed sadism returns. In another variant of this process, one patient controlled his aggressiveness by adopting a passive, ineffectual role in work, in his studies, and in heterosexual relations. He would bring about his failure academically, sometimes limiting his activity almost to the point of inertness.

Here, too, the repressed sadism returned in the form of disappointing his mother and wife with failures and unassertiveness.

The central importance of the phallic mother fantasy for the male subject has been discussed in Chapter II. We noted that when confronted with the seemingly castrated woman, the young boy—through a process of perceptual distortion—"repairs" her image by endowing it with a penis in order to make the mother seem less terrifying. The initial fearfulness toward the woman, however, can break through this defensive strategem, since the early phallic mother image remains far more vivid than the idealized, madonna-like figure of puberty. The adult homosexual male is unable to contend with the female genital either in its actuality or with the fantasy reparation.

Elements of humiliation and degradation seem to be common, though not universal, characteristics in perverse fantasy and activity. On one level, the masochistic experience may be viewed as a repetition compulsion with two contradictory objectives: overcoming and mastering a sadistic attack while, at the same time, submitting to it. On another level, the act of submission can be interpreted as an expiating gesture which atones for sadistic impulses toward the parent.

In some perversions, the man requires that he be humiliated by his partner. Even more frequently, however, he wishes to humiliate her—a sequence that may terminate in abusive and savage genital coitus.

In one patient studied by the group, the members viewed the need-to-be-beaten function from a variety of perspectives (Case IV):

1. The beating represented an infantile and erotized punishment for having superseded his father and brothers and for the enjoyment of prohibited sexual impulses.

2. It represented a masochistic wish to identify with the castrated woman: the patient retained a childhood feminine self-image and felt that, by identifying with the woman, he could achieve rebirth.

3. By generating sexual excitement, it revived flagging potency which could then be used for heterosexual intercourse or could itself be enjoyed as a sensual experience.

4. It served to reproduce a significant infantile experience.

5. It was a defensive inversion of a wish to attack the woman sadistically.

Thus, the need to be beaten can be seen as the expression of a passive libidinal need and a wish to be reborn—both id functions; as a defense against phallic aggressiveness—an ego function; or, it may be a need for punishment and an expiation of guilt—a superego function. The need derives its strength from the fact that it serves all three agencies at the same time.

The underlying structuring of behavior, shaped by specific experiences in early development, is designed to facilitate the discharge of erotic and aggressive impulses through an "action-resolution" of the individual cluster of instinctual conflicts and anxieties.

In general, the cases studied by the group indicated that three elements were major factors in facilitating perverse gratifications: (1) the adoption of any type of ritual action or any special kind of equipment; (2) escape from influence of the superego; and (3) regression of ego function and libidinal disposition.

In several of the instances studied, the individual perverse experience consisted of two discrete phases. In the first phase, the person engages in the specific perverse act which has special meaning for the individual and is pregenital in character. It elicits sexual excitement but has specific defensive significance as well. In some instances—especially in masochistic perversions—the behavior serves first to expiate guilt. In many forms of perversion it alleviates castration anxiety by creating the illusion that the woman possesses a penis. It also, in some cases, seems designed to gratify feminine fantasies.

The essential by-product of the initial phase in perverse activity is to make the man more potent. He then employs this potency in the second phase of the sexual episode—relatively normal heterosexual intercourse. It is uncertain whether the first phase is a *necessary* preparation for the second, or whether the second phase serves merely as a final common discharge path for the first.

The observation that many women achieve satisfaction only via the orgasm of their partners and forfeit direct satisfaction of their own suggests that genital discharge is not always necessary. It has been relatively difficult for the study group to obtain case material dealing with perversions of women. The previous chapter indicated some of the possible factors accounting for the differences between men and women in the dynamics of perverse behavior—reasons which are largely attributable to differences in childhood experience.

In reporting on female homosexuality, one member noted that the oedipal problem assumed prominence in each case. Available preoedipal material represented only regressive retreat from the oedipal conflict. Two elements seemed important: (1) the girl's wish to be the boy whom the father would have preferred; and, (2) a reaction formation against an intensive competitive relation with the mother or older sister.

Overall, culture conspires to make the woman less needful of the solution represented by overt perversion. In Western society the woman is typically permitted greater erotization of her body than the man, and also greater erotization in the choice of clothing. In this way, she achieves—without appearing deviant—more pregenital gratification than does the man. In addition, women may find a culturally generated satisfaction in accepting and participating in the mode of sexual gratification preferred by their partners.

Several other factors may contribute to this difference. The woman cannot "fail" in intercourse, in the sense of being unable to participate in the physical requirements of the act. She does not require a threshold level of excitement, as does her partner, and therefore she need not flee to a perverse act from fear of failure.

Many women take comfort in the fantasy that they possess a penis—often, one that is concealed intravaginally. The existence of the "hidden" penis cannot be challenged in intercourse in any visible way, so that intercourse represents no denial of the fantasy.

We assume that women are, to one degree or another, disappointed with the female genital (although this assumption is no longer unequivocally subscribed to by all psychoanalysts). Even before they have developed a mature adult sexuality, the tendency has been to favor displacement of sexual sensitivity to other organs. Thus, the woman normally participates in intercourse more diffusely than the man, whose feelings and sensations are centered much more closely on the genital.

The woman can, in effect, "smuggle" her pregenital needs into her daily life without betraying any obvious deviation. Play with children offers an additional source of sensual gratification. She can find gratification for her pregenital oral dependent needs for the mother in a passive sexual role in heterosexuality. Unlike the man, then, she does not need to create a sub rosa pattern of perverse activities and is not driven to replicate earlier experiences with the mother.

Dr. Valenstein called attention to the fundamental changes rapidly taking place in Western society which have tended to reduce the differences in behavior expectations between women and men. He does not anticipate that, as a result of these changes, men will become less fearful of castration. However, he suggests that women may tend to see less advantage in possessing a penis, although the basic biologic difference may be so profound that its effects cannot be nullified by even the most radical social change. On the other hand, sociocultural changes may ultimately produce an increase in the incidence of overt sexual perversion among women.

Chapter IV
THE EGO

Since the etiology and dynamics of perverse behavior have been examined so intensively in the past, most members of the group anticipated the study of ego function in sexual perversion would be particularly productive.

The first of the ego function factors to be explored was perceptual "hypersensitivity." The material presented indicated that many patients—particularly male homosexuals—demonstrated an unusual sensitivity to visual stimulation.

The basis of this sensitivity was not clear, but it obviously played a significant role in many aspects of the perverse pattern. Constitutional elements provide a psychophysiologic basis for the characteristic, leading to the possibility that this faculty could be viewed either as an autonomous ego function or as a sublimation of a previously erotized ego function. It may also be derived from a powerfully intensified sexual drive which heightens the visual factor in the *service* of the total ego structure of the perverse personality.

An ethological observation introduced by Dr. Ostow may be analogously productive in this speculation. Intensification of drive pressure in certain animal species lowers the threshold for the response to specific "releasing configurations." As the drive becomes stronger, percepts that differ more and more from the ideal achieve releasing value. In this sense the tolerance for objects that deviate from the biologically ideal might be considered a function of impulse strength.

A provocative research observation noted by Dr. Gero, in this connection, was that eidetic imagery seems to be part "reality" and part fantasy. It has the vividness and persuasiveness of actual visual perception but can, according to some studies, be altered according to emotional needs.

Whatever the source, this capacity appears to permit a visual incorporative identification—a "merging"—with the desired object, and is effective in relation to a variety of other ego functions. By looking at an athletic man, for example, one patient felt that he became like that man—virile, lithe, similarly endowed with a "magnificent" penis. By visually incorporating the penis of his partner, the homosexual male is apparently enabled to identify with an idealized or magnificent phallic father, thereby attaining full virility.

The purposeful interaction of a hypersensitive perceptivity, the magical incorporation, and the patient's defensive pattern were concisely elucidated by Dr. Arlow:

> First, there was some kind of autonomous endowment in the man, who was perceptually very acute. Secondly, under the impact of conflict and the regression of ego function, this perceptual acuity combined with an earlier modality of ego functioning—namely, the tendency to identify with what one perceived. These two factors then worked together to buttress an unconscious fantasy of getting the necessary power from an omnipotent father figure and using it in situations in which he felt threatened.

The role of the perceptual system in the ego structure of many perverse patients was dramatically illustrated in a case in which the patient—who engaged in a variety of polymorphous perverse experiences—would peer into the vagina of his partner for long periods of time. Once he had stopped looking—searching, that is, for the illusory penis—the patient could no longer "remember" what he had seen, and repeated the procedure. Another case was reported in connection with the capacity to summon up extremely vivid visual images. This patient—who had vaginal anesthesia but a very active fantasy life of a perverse character—reached orgasm by visualizing a penis inside her body.

This extraordinary capacity for visualization also appeared in a case in which there was no manifest perversion. The patient had entered analysis because of marital problems. At the time, he was involved with another woman and planned to leave his wife in order to marry her—a decision he later abandoned. He had no complaints against his wife, and they both enjoyed their four children.

The symptom that particularly bothered this patient was an inability to achieve orgasm or ejaculation without the use of fantasy. This inability occurred both in his marriage relation and in his extramarital affair. In order to complete the sexual act, he had to visualize a tall, attractive nude woman. If one image did not excite him enough, he would substitute a taller fantasy woman. The fantasy did not involve the sexual act: in effect, the man had to visualize a still picture of a nude. Here, in an apparently normal man, was a classic voyeuristic and fetishistic perversion which became the sine qua non for the orgasm.

At times, every sensory modality was involved in the perverse subject's pattern of structured behavior. In one case discussed by the group (Case II), a male homosexual indulged in a sequence of engagements from fanciful to actual object: from pure fantasy, to visual stimulation through photographs, to telephone contact—until the final act of involvement with another man at a gymnasium.

In another case (Case VI), involving zoophilia, the patient also attempted to incorporate the object through the use of several sensory modalities, but the incorporation was almost psychotic, in the sense that he wished to *become* the object rather than to *become like* him. Exhibiting fluid ego boundaries, the patient sought to achieve this merging through concrete, lived experiences. He exhibited a spectrum of perverse characteristics some of which were present in other cases explored by the group: erotization of the perceptual system, unusual eidetic capacity, an absence of stable object relations during the early years.

Dr. Rappaport suggested that the excess of libidinization was actually an attempt to make up for the lack of mothering. In his opinion, for this patient particularly, the combination of the lack of mothering and the father's attempt to take over the mother's role was the basis of the patient's perverse development.

In many instances the ability to distort perceived reality was utilized to give concreteness to the image of the phallic mother and to achieve a fancied mastery of the object. The male homosexual was almost literally able to "see" an illusory penis when viewing the female genital. Boys who must submit to overwhelmingly domineering mothers may call upon and develop eidetic-type visualization and nurture perceptual distortion in an attempt to control the one area of experience that can remain private—the domain of fantasy.

The process of "merging" also has a tactile dimension. Dr. Gero explored the dynamics of this behavior:

> When the mother went to work, the boy would put on her nightgown. This was more than identification—it was an effort at merging. It also related to the matter of tension tolerance, in that the child could not bear the tension which the mother's absence precipitated and attempted to reestablish a unity through her clothing. This manifestation of a transvestite inclination clearly related to tactile eroticism as the sensory vehicle.

The second aspect of ego function in perversion that the study group considered was the compelling need to act. This predilection for action is more than simply a tendency to "act out." Acting-out is primarily a means of circumventing conflict by engaging in an activity whose true meaning is denied, and in which short-term gratification is generally obtained at the expense of ultimate defeat. The perverse individual does act out, but for him, action—in contrast with contemplation—is, quite literally, a way of life.

Many male patients, particularly homosexuals, are characteristically limited in their capacity for abstract thought, and in compensation, appear to cultivate their perceptual hypersensitivity. The need to act and to do complements the hypercathexis of perception, and the combined characteristics enhance a tendency to seek the literalness and concreteness of experience. Since abstract thought is not a "natural" or satisfying mode, he must become involved—in a vitally immediate sense—with feeling and doing. The typically low toleration for frustration also contributes to this drive to action.

Most of the speculation concerning perverse acting or acting-out has revolved about the issue of castration anxiety. But the qualitative difference and "quantum jump" between fantasy and action almost certainly involve other sources of anxiety as well as a persistent dynamic factor. This dynamic factor, as noted by Dr. Arlow, may be a two-element "condition" that makes both necessary and possible the transformation of fantasy into the reality of the act. The individual may be impelled to act when (a) fantasy does not provide gratification; and (b) a seduction-like experience or actual seduction in childhood has provided the framework for the act.

This actual experience, proposed Dr. Valenstein, structures and patterns the need for discharge through doing. The event—or series of events—affects the perceptual aspect of the action system at an early developmental stage, and when the child is overcathecting. As a result, the action response becomes a magical rectification, a method by which the perverse adult copes with a frustrating and/or anxiety-producing reality.

Dr. Valenstein suggested that some confluence of ego functions in the perverse personality informs the quality of experience so that it overcathects both the action and the perceptual systems. The person's perverse predilections are in some manner converted into a response pattern that serves as a defense against, for example, castration anxiety. These factors, particularly when "bound" to an early seduction trauma and in combination with conflictual elements, seem to give rise to an ego structure vis-à-vis the instincts that facilitates the breakthrough of an impulse in the form of action.

In the perverse patient, Dr. Arlow observed, concrete representations of impulses were frequently organized into a very articulate fantasy, with a tendency to convert that fantasy into a certain type of action. A critical issue in perversion is how this dynamic configuration differs fundamentally from the individual with an impulse disorder. According to Dr. Gero, the dominant role of fantasy in the sex life, in association with the need to achieve *literal* forms of gratification, appears to be a primary characteristic in clinical perversion.

The "literalness" of the ego structure, its roots in a primitive concreteness, along with shifting boundaries of images of self and objects and changing states, observes Dr. Blos, occur commonly in varying types of perverse personalities.

Two issues, equally complex and central to an understanding of ego function in perversion, crystallized out of these considerations:

> 1. The nature of developmental patterns with respect to the ego's readiness to permit instinctual gratification; and
> 2. The dynamics of the action pattern, and whether they typically suggest a focus of fixation and/or regression.

In Dr. Valenstein's view, an instinctual thrust, triggered by an incestuous relationship, by early and generalized sexual activity, or in a specific seduction trauma, then forced a premature consolidation of a sense of sexual inadequacy or impairment. This early impression was fixed, probably at an unconscious level, leaving a residual conviction that the individual is unable to function sexually without the intervention of a magical event. Such fixed ideas are unresponsive to the actuality of masculine development over the years.

The ability to obtain the powerful phallus and potency through corporeal and visual incorporation was frequently accompanied by this severely impaired body-image. Dr. Blos notes that virtually all of the male homosexuals that he has treated have been convinced that their penises were smaller than "normal."

The group proposed that the development of body-image was, in large measure, a function of the nature of object relations and that, in particular, the child's image of his body was initially created and cathected in response to the mother's care. Examples ranged from a young male who developed phantom breasts that he could "feel" after humiliating and threatening experiences with girls, to a child who was so dissociated from his body that he drew people whose body parts were operated by strings.

In Dr. Gero's view, the action pattern need not be focused on a point of fixation and facilitated by frustration of gratification in normal discharge channels. The ego structure, he observed, can permit a regressive return to a concrete, fetishistic, part-object relationship.

"The point of fixation to which the individual regresses," Dr. Ostow commented, "appears to be related to the specific inhibition involved." In Case I, he noted that, "an inhibition of hostile wishes towards the patient's wife resulted in a regression to a mode of

dealing with hostility utilized in childhood. Here, a voluptuous element was also introduced which apparently replaced the sexual
pleasure that was not achieved with the wife. The patient was angry
with his wife and could not obtain sexual gratification with her,
so he regressed to a childhood form of anger with the mother and,
at the same time, recaptured some of the sensuality missing in
his relations with his wife."

In support of this observation, Dr. Ostow observed that in
perversion, as in normal behavior, some type of object relation was
associated with orgasm. It is the *nature* of the object relation and
the *identity* of the object that distinguishes the perverse act from
the normal. In perversion, regression is a necessary condition for
adequate sexual discharge, and sexual pleasure is inhibited when
regression does not take place. Clearly, the route for discharge—
structured by instinctual and developmental factors—could be both
fixated by an early trauma and facilitated by libidinal and ego
regression.

The consensus of the group, then, was that action in the perverse individual is impelled because fantasy gratification proves
inadequate and is further favored if an actual event in childhood
provides material for a magical replication through action (doing
makes it so). Action may also be facilitated by a variety of other
specific arousing and fixating experiences—for example, an excessively intimate relation between the patient and his parents. Also,
when both libidinal and aggressive impulses strive for gratification
at the same time, fantasy is more likely to be transformed into action.
As stated by Dr. Arlow: "There is a tendency or need to try simultaneously to obtain sexual gratification and to handle an overwhelming amount of aggression. A perverse action makes possible a 'solution' that will gratify both conflicting tendencies at once."

This aspect of perversion was strikingly illustrated in the case
of a male homosexual with concurrent libidinous and aggressive
drives toward horses (Case VI). Dr. Furst commented:

> The horse was not only an erotic object but also the object of
> an aggressive impulse. The patient petted the horse but wished
> to strangle it, to castrate it. This behavior was in accord with
> many of our points about perversion, particularly concerning the
> male homosexual, for whom part of the attraction to the object

with a large penis was that he could steal it and, in depriving him of it, magically possess it for his very own. A tolerance for inconsistency was also indicated when the same object was both an erotic object and the focus of aggression.

A formulation proposed by Dr. Gero was that the individual normally has instinctual impulses which give rise to unconscious fantasy. In the striving for gratification, the fantasy moves to the conscious level. In the case of perversion, however, the subject cannot tolerate the intervention of conscious awareness at this phase; he must act out the unconscious fantasy to convert it directly into reality. In the service of this objective, secondary process is bypassed.

Other observations by the study group concerning the perverse subject's predilection for action were that he is likely to have been an overactive infant and an extremely active child; that this proclivity may in part be constitutional; but may also be a response to the mother's encouragement and/or demands, as well as an imitation of an active mother. Doing—particularly in terms of the body, and with less restraint than in other individuals—becomes a magical method for solving problems. The early behavioral pattern often suggests that it is not so important *what* is done, as it is that *something* is done.

A characteristic fundamental to each of the perverse patients studied by the group was the capacity to tolerate inconsistency more readily than do others. This quality appears to be a specific type of ego weakness: a facility for entertaining contradictory sentiments and opposing drives at the same time.

Dr. Sterba referred to Anna Freud's comment that two- and three-year-old children are capable of sustaining drive ambivalence, noting that when ego integration takes place, one of the contradictory drives must be repressed. However, Dr. Arlow asserted that that characteristic, though it is an ego quality that may *permit* or encourage the perversion to flourish, should probably not be considered a *driving force* in perversion.

The tolerance for inconsistency—which was related to Freud's description of the split ego of the fetishist—may represent a developmental defect: The perverse personality not only tolerates both genitality and pregenitality, he exploits inconsistent and multiple identifications, thus sustaining both realistic as well as severely distorted perceptions. The patient maintains this tolerance by denial and, if the denial is challenged, may in some instances resist therapy or possibly lapse into serious psychotic regression.

As a consequence of his ability to entertain opposing points of view about the same object or event, the patient is enabled to enjoy his perverse activities because they are literal, concrete, and real, and at the same time he can think of them as a game that can be interrupted at will. He is, therefore, willing to tolerate anxiety-provoking situations, passivity, humiliation and degradation, since he "knows" that they are not "real." One particularly clear-cut example of such behavior was that of a patient who playfully "seduced" a prostitute into mutually degrading behavior and, at the same time, required that she give evidence of approval of his actions so that her pleasure—as a form of game-playing—masked his aggressive need (Case I).

In specific perverse activities the patient often repeats and reproduces in a "play mode" the very urgent and often threatening experiences of early childhood. The idea of utilizing a "game" in this way may itself be an outgrowth of games that the patient played with his parents as a child.

There was substantial evidence that when the game is "spoiled" and the situation gets out of hand—when, for example, the partner will not follow instructions necessary for an effective magical replication, or when the danger that has been precipitated moves out of control—the pleasure is marred and anxiety appears. This prospect notwithstanding, the patient is constantly tempted to make the perverse situation increasingly realistic—which might well mean increasingly dangerous—because his pleasure is, in part, a function of the degree of excitement he experiences.

Here, too, the games of childhood—although clearly identified as such—appear to exert a profound influence. Thus, the perverse reenactment ritual has two fundamental aspects: the *realistic*—which produces excitement and provides gratification, and the *make-believe*—which offers defense against anxiety.

Although the perverse person requires some sort of object relation and does not "deny" the reality of the external world, as do some psychotics, paradoxically he turns his back on reality; or, at least, he insists on distorting it within a significantly and highly specific constellation. At times, the process leading to perversion commences with a form of abandonment of the real world, much as it does in the case of schizophrenia. The perverse act becomes, in this sense, an act of restitution, an effort to reestablish object relationships according to highly idiosyncratic constructions. In fact, since the object of the perversion often represents the *self*, the patient is protecting himself against further disappointment by what is essentially a narcissistic retreat very much like that of the schizophrenic.

In the only case of child perversion that was studied, the group found that the child's image of his parents' roles was unclear and inconstant. Here, the child's self-image was equally disturbed. These complementary disturbances were related to a number of factors. The identity and roles of family members were distorted and "concealed." A mysterious atmosphere was used by the family as a life-style mystique, and was clearly designed to obscure reality. The parents competed with the children and with each other. Father and mother played paternal and maternal roles interchangeably, with obvious ambivalence toward the children. They exhibited extremes of seductiveness, passivity, and aggression, and themselves acted out deviant psychosexual needs. Since the parents presented no consistent, clearly delineated and differentiated role images, the child developed two sets of personality traits, each representing one of the parents. A hermaphroditic self-image developed that was congruent with the image of the phallic mother (Case III).

In a marriage where both husband and wife exhibit strong perverse tendencies or actual perversions, we often find that a child is drawn into a conspiracy to ignore some aspect of reality—to promote an unrealistic attitude; to behave, in fact, in a psychotic way toward a specific feature of family life usually having to do with the sex life within the household. It was also suggested that in the ego structure of the perverse patient, there is often a nuclear fantasy that remains untouched by reality testing. Around it, material of a sexual nature clusters. In such cases, family sanction in some manner permits the release of this material from repression so that it becomes accepted by the patient as a part of the real world. It seems to be a recapitulation of the original primary narcissism, which persists even after the illusion of infantile omnipotence is yielded to the idealized object.

Family secrets seem to create highly charged nuclear fantasies of this kind and often lead to delinquency as well as to perverse action. In the area influenced by this fantasy, the patient's sense of reality was severely and fundamentally distorted.

In the cases examined by the study group, patients tended to form relations in a primitive way, with part objects rather than whole objects. Dr. Blos observed that the ego never really progressed to a synthesis—a postambivalence synthesis—of the whole object. Sexual pleasure was obtained only in relation to the part object. This deficit in ego structure gave the perverse act its compelling character. Since progress from part- to whole-object representation is required for the resolution of ambivalence, in perversion the ambivalence is never really conquered.

All these qualities of ego function in perversion facilitate the illusion of omnipotence. Clearly evident in the child case, the sense of omnipotence was encouraged by a conspiracy to overlook reality and to impress a pseudoreality upon the family's fantasy world.

As mentioned earlier, since the perverse male considers the penis to be a weapon of murderous potential, he controls its action by becoming impotent or through a homosexual relation. The omnipotent patient must feel not only that he can destroy the object at will, but that he can also rescue it from destruction. Ordinarily, this assumption of omnipotence in an adult is limited to the area of sexuality. In the child case, however, to the extent that the patient's ego weakness enabled him to alter the image of the real world, it also made it possible for him to alter the image of his own body. He thus grew up with an ambiguous sexual self-image which could be made to conform to the needs of the moment, using prosthetic devices to alter or to distort his sexual image—making it now more male, now more female.

In one of its case presentations, the group found the widest range and largest number of elements adduced throughout its sessions as being specific indicators of perversion (Case I). The patient, fraught with unresolved oedipal conflict and laden with castration anxiety, came into analysis ostensibly because of a poor and deteriorating marital relationship. An enumeration of this patient's characteristics should provide a useful summary of the dynamic factors and ego qualities that appear to be fundamental to perversion.

For this patient, the perverse act provided gratification because:

1. through it he acted out a confrontation of idealized and degraded images of his mother;

2. it gratified sadistic and masochistic wishes that were otherwise unacceptable;

3. castration anxiety and guilt—which he would ordinarily experience in the sexual relation—were successfully warded off by the perverse defensive system;

4. the element of the "game" in the perverse act concealed an inner primary-process conviction that the experience was indeed real and serious;

5. the perversion acted out a forbidden wish in disguised form—specifically, both the oedipal wish and the homosexual transference;

6. it reenacted the primal scene;

7. it also reenacted childhood seduction and gratification by the parents;

8. it permitted actual gratification by an actual substitute object, so that the anxiety of object loss was allayed;

9. it stimulated sexual desire and potency, permitting the perverse episode to be consummated with an act of heterosexual intercourse as an epilogue.

Chapter V
THE SUPEREGO

In perversion, the influence of the superego is frequently nullified through the ego's tolerance for inconsistency. In addition, in most perverse individuals the superego itself has developed imperfectly.

In male homosexuality, for example, the patient has failed to internalize his ego ideal. He is compelled to seek it elsewhere, and selects as his partner an individual in whom it is personified: the partner is the representation of what he would like to be. In such cases, where there is a specific inhibition in the superego formation and an arrest at a stage of hypercathexis of the male organ, there is an erotization of the organ through displacement to a specific object that represents it.

During the course of his maturation, then, the perverse individual fails to develop a superego through the normal process of identification with the parent. Instead, there is a form of narcissistic *merging* with the early image of the parent—that is, a regression to a point antecedent to the child's establishment of clear-cut boundaries between self and mother; to a nonverbal, experience-structured stage before the point at which the superego would ordinarily become dominant.

This process of merging is commonly reflected in the perverse act. For example, the man looks at the image of a woman with large breasts and becomes stimulated by the sense of merging with her. The mechanism appears to be facilitated by the tendency to relate to part objects rather than to the whole object—to the breast rather than to the woman; paramountly a narcissistic orientation to objects.

There is substantial indication that this process in perversion repeats what had been a frequent and familiar pattern during early development. At times the narcissistic merging alternates with the need for a concretely gratifying relation with the parent. When this kind of relation is reestablished in the transference, it binds the patient to the analyst, but at the same time it may render the analyst's interpretations ineffectual unless the analysis of transference material is carried out vigorously and consistently.

In terms of unresolved transference material, one case history indicated that the superego influence of the analyst was utilized by the patient—via an interpretation of the patient's rage at his mother—to obtain "permission" to engage in overt homosexual activity (Case II). The patient was constantly self-critical and, through a cluster of concerns related to what he felt was inadequate memory, developed a superego-induced "composite" symptom. Though at times there seemed to be effective superego intervention, Dr. Ostow pointed out that the issue was not the occasional presence of a strict superego, but the *stability* of superego function:

> The fact that there is sometimes a strict superego does not mean that at other times the superego does not become lax. In the classical picture of manic-depressive psychosis, the individual may at one point permit himself to be 'murdered' by the superego and, at another time, repudiate it completely. In a sense, the strictness of the superego *per se* indicates nothing about its stability.

In elaborating upon this issue, Dr. Arlow commented:

> A superego cannot be categorized as being strong, strict, weak, etc. Conglomerate sets of functions operate, and even in the most obsessional person, certain demands are met in one way while other demands are met in quite a different way. The superego functions

are quite distinct and discrete and it is not possible to generalize from the evidence of minute attitudes.

In many instances, the individual reinforces narcissistic gratification by merging with one parent, while at the same time using the primitive type of identification with the other. For example, the homosexual boy may augment his self-love by feeling united with his mother; by becoming his mother. At the same time, however, he presents no threat to the father and he consequently feels able to establish a gratifying relation with him. A variant of this process appears to be involved in the case of homosexual development through *double* identification—when the son "remains loyal" to the mother by not relating to another woman.

True superego formation does not derive from this kind of archaic identification; there is no *integration* of the cultural substructure on which the parent's superego is partly based. It essentially involves, instead, an *imitation* of the parent's superficial qualities and traits. The child clearly fails to identify with the parent's superego; he may even reject identification with the parent's superego because of feelings of anger toward him.

This process was exemplified in a case outlined briefly for the group. The patient's father constantly humiliated the mother, and the patient's complete libidinal life was invested in sado-masochistic fantasies. She represented a classic union of erotization with aggression, structured by the fact that the original object of the hatred— the father—was also the object of the love. In this case, the patient literally gratified her oedipal wishes: she replaced the mother as her father's closest companion. Faced with continuing evidence of her mother's humiliation, it became vital that, on a conscious level, she demonstrate her superiority. The more fundamental wish, however, was to replace her mother as the degraded object. The breakthrough of that wish—the event that initiated her illness and brought her into analysis—was the patient's removal of all her clothing to scrub the floor in her home.

In this context, Dr. Furst suggested that the specific perverse pattern "owed its origin to the fact that one of the patient's parents had been so manifestly and consistently degraded that degradation as a perversion became internalized in the superego." "If," Dr. Kanzer observed, "the object was a debased representation of a portion of the superego—if, in fact, the object who represented the superego were discovered in the sex act itself—then its authority could be dethroned. By contrast, the condemnation ordinarily in operation in the creation of neurotic symptoms was based on the fact that the superego retained its authority."

The group's case material also suggested, according to Dr. Valenstein, that in certain perversions "an important component of the superego is located *externally*; the superego has not been thoroughly internalized, enabling the person to 'buy in' on special permission and sanction. This phenomenon seems to operate through the 'auxiliary superego' as represented by a prostitute, perhaps, and indicates a developmental defect at an early stage."

The perverse individual escapes the influence of the superego in a number of ways—it may be evaded, bribed, ignored, or over-thrown. The perverse person's degradation of the object may represent a *debasing* of a portion of the superego, the superego object, or, the perversion may become overt simply because superego integration is ineffective, in which case the perverse patient may demand gratification whenever the need arises. In this respect, he resembles children and artists; both groups typically base their standards of behavior upon a primitive, merging type of identification with a parent, rather than upon response to true superego influence.

The influence of the superego is easily discerned in the perverse act. For example, part of the perverse ritual might require that the individual deliberately refrain from touching a part of his own body or a part of his partner's body. Some individuals insist that their hands be bound, as if in response to a superego prohibition against using their hands improperly. Where the penis is alternately jeopardized and then "rescued," the ritual clearly provides reassurance against castration. In one such case, in which the patient tied his scrotum and handcuffed himself, Dr. Ostow inferred that "superego involvement was indicated by a need to demonstrate that the genital was not endangered by punishment even though it was used as a source of pleasure."

Superego influence might also become manifest in the occasional catastrophic outcome. An individual might start a perverse or homosexual adventure with the intention of merely courting danger, but he might lose control over the situation and ultimately be mutilated or killed.

The patient in Case I feared that he might have been poisoned by a drop of urine that entered his stomach. This is an example of "superego literalization." The patient in this case required a prostitute to urinate on him. His mother had died of accidental ingestion of a poisonous substance.

The role of the superego tends, according to Dr. Ostow, to emphasize the distinction between neurosis—which has strong superego components—and perversion, which often involves pre-superego dynamics, but which may include a masochistic element through secondary use of the superego.

Masochistic acts were, in part, attributed to the need for punishment for oedipal wishes, but the masochistic element in the perverse act may also have been an expiation of guilt as a necessary prelude to genital gratification. A dramatic example of how the perverse act functions as a magical expiation of guilt was provided the group in the case of a patient who suddenly developed a need to be beaten several times each day (Case IV). The patient described himself as a "double murderer": he had taken over his father's role of pater familias, and had married a woman who resembled the fiancée of another brother, who had been killed in an accident.

How does it happen that the individual permits the perversion to be carried to the point of injury? Generally, the patient tries to arrest the process if he fears that he is losing control over it. However, since the anxiety itself is libidinized, the momentum of the dangerous activity may override the normal self-preservative tendencies of the ego. If he exerts too much control over the perverse act, the subject will diminish the danger but may also diminish the degree of pleasurable excitement that it provides.

The influence of the superego also becomes manifest in the aftermath of the perverse act. Many perverse individuals may enjoy the act without suffering negative feelings after its completion. In fact, as suggested earlier, one might define a "successful" perversion as one in which the performance of the desired act creates a feeling of relief. However, as noted in Chapter III, although some perverse acts are calculated to take advantage of the stimulating effects of anxiety, anxiety may escape from control or itself be generated by the perverse behavior. Anxiety may result from fear of superego retribution, as well as from fear of danger that is realistically present. In addition, the patient may fear punishment through bodily injury because he believes that he deserves it, and because he has precipitated a situation that is, in fact, dangerous.

The most common negative aftermath of perversion is a feeling of remorse, a mixture of shame and guilt. Certainly, guilt is present in many instances, although several members of the group believed that feelings of shame overshadowed guilt. The ratio between the two can, perhaps, be correlated with the proportion of pregenital to aggressive components in the perverse act itself.

Chapter VI
THE TREATMENT
OF PERVERSION

From the outset, the study group was aware that perverse individuals who come to the attention of the analyst are, virtually by definition, not "content," much less at peace with their perversion. By expressing an explicit desire for therapeutic assistance, this segment of the perverse population exhibits characteristics that almost certainly distinguish it from those whose need-gratification encounters relatively little ego or superego resistance. Some homosexuals and some individuals with other types of perversions "enjoy" their perverse behavior with relatively little anxiety or guilt.

Clearly, then, individuals who come into analysis are those whose gratification is in some manner diluted or negated by anxiety and conflict. The assumption can be made, in these cases, that one basic aspect of the patient's personality is not optimally functional in the structuring of perverse behavior so as to achieve gratification and a reconciliation of opposing drives. What is lacking, the group has conjectured, is *ego compliance:* a fundamental and wide tolerance for inconsistency flowing from an essential ego weakness.

The structuring of action in the patient is, according to Dr. Valenstein, the core of the analytic challenge. The dynamics on which it is based represent both the most effective site for therapeutic intervention and the core of patient resistance. Dr. Valenstein observed:

> The most complex aspect of the problem is that insofar as there is a strong pleasure component in the orgasm and its associated gratification, the action that has been experientially channeled to discharge in this manner is likely to continue. This active, experiential structure suggests that an action-oriented form of therapy may be effective. It is, then, not surprising that those who wished to move beyond the limitations of the psychoanalytic method—Ferenczi, Rank, Reich—entered into, in some respects, the discharge—or structured life pattern—of their patients.
>
> There is clearly something about the magic of perception and action which is of central importance here, and which makes the behavior both possible and gratifying. This structure, of course, is what we attempt to undo in our analysis. The first step is to begin to rob the perceptual system of its magic, producing concomitant changes in the action-discharge pattern and lessening the ability to tolerate conflict.

In the broadest sense, the perverse patient's application for treatment can be viewed as an effort to solve—in a less conflicting and anxiety-producing manner—the very problem which originally produced a pattern of deviant behavior.

Although the immediate antecedent event that propels the patient into analysis may or may not be related to a particular perverse act or episode, soon after the analysis begins it usually becomes evident that the underlying pathology involves a disturbance in object relations of one or several of the types discussed in Chapter II. The variety of "triggering" events and anxieties that can lead to a request for analysis was fully exemplified in the cases presented to the study group. Two of the histories—Cases I and IV —indicate the range of such antecedent incidents or disturbances, as well as the explicit or masked character of the problem. In one, the patient was concerned about a deteriorating marital relation; in the other, the patient found that he had suddenly developed a wish to be beaten.

Within the framework of the analysis itself, transference dynamics typically reproduce vital aspects of the other object relation patterns. As Dr. Ostow noted, "in the vicissitudes of the transference, a recapitulation of the patient's history of object relations can usually be observed."

In the case of a patient (Case V) who would often seem to fall asleep during sessions, the group related his behavior to the passive seduction that he utilized in homosexual contacts. Dr. Kanzer commented: "His virtually going to sleep was equivalent to an invitation to explore him. At some point in his life there was this sharp switch from the positive temper tantrums and sexual outlets, into a defensive denial, a passive way of allowing somebody to do what he wanted them to do. At the point at which his own active impulses were going to come out, he relapsed into a passive, feminine type of action and tried to impel others into undertaking actively what he wanted."

Since the transference in the analysis of the perverse patient tends to become so libidinized and inordinately complex, it is often difficult to assess. One day the patient wishes the analyst to be the mother; the next, to be the father. If fantasy involves the analyst as father, it is frequently replaced with other wish images because the patient cannot tolerate that relation, either.

When the analyst fails to provide consistent solace, the patient may withdraw, replacing whatever gratification has been provided in the analysis with narcissistically achieved gratification. This substitution, however, ultimately becomes equally intolerable since it exacerbates the initial anxiety and reactivates the loneliness and conflict of the preanalytic period.

Dr. Rappaport pointed out that a typical maneuver of the patient with an erotized transference is teasing, which he attempts to turn into mutual teasing in order to force the competitor (analyst, father, object) to fall into a rage (representing orgasm, ejaculation). Thus the teasing patient, by throwing the object into a rage, acquires his powers. The analyst must keep this maneuver in mind and refuse to react with anger to the patient's persistent provocation.

The fluid ego boundaries characteristic of perversion present a major resistance factor in the analysis. The patient's frequent identity shifts often make interpretation relatively ineffective, and the analyst faces the continuing problem of determining which aspect of the ego should be addressed; how to find the "real" self that encapsulates the essential unwillingness to accept the perverse solution and provides the thrust towards change. An important element in the resistance of the patient to interpretation, Dr. Kanzer suggested, stems from this difficulty of "localizing" where the authentic "self-feeling" is concealed, especially as the self-image is so paradoxically not one, but two or several, isolated one from another.

Since role playing, as noted earlier, is a vital aspect of perverse behavior—most clearly in action-replications of the primal scene—at such times the patient is not "himself," but the father or mother. As a result, interpretations are not "really" concerned with the patient. In this way, according to Drs. Blos and Kanzer, a particular interpretation may be directed to the presently manifesting pseudo-self, without reaching the core self in the total ego organization. It is the process of dealing with the multiple shadow selves and of providing interpretations that effectively touch the more substantially mature, reality-oriented self that can produce progress. "In effect," Dr. Ostow concluded, "the central therapeutic task is to utilize sources of anxiety and guilt while exposing the unconscious wish and the extraordinary use of denial—often revolving about the oedipal relation—that is the substructure of the perversion."

Though perverse patients frequently exhibit almost intuitive and immediate grasp of the symbolic form and meaning of material, they may not respond to, and progress through, its interpretation. The reason, Dr. Ostow suggested, is that for these persons it is not the symbolic *meaning* that has been repressed. What has been repressed is the recognition of the *primary object relation* from which the symbolic meaning arises. Since this relation is often the fulcrum of resistance, it becomes the central focus of the analysis.

The analyst can attempt to overcome the patient's extraordinary tolerance of conflict and inconsistency by the introduction of environmental intolerance. He can, for example, reinforce a weak superego protest by drawing constant attention to potential or actual embarrassing, threatening, or harmful consequences of the behavior. Or, the analyst may elect to suggest that the patient spend some time in a hospital which will provide more effective and structural control of external factors.

It may be productive to undertake a frontal approach by

explicitly prohibiting the gratification indulgence. This approach must, however, be utilized with great caution. Not only does this polarize the transference, verifying superego expectations and anxiety, but, in the case where the perversion is literally the patient's "last-ditch" defense against severe depression, psychosis, and disintegration, such a prohibition may precipitate massive resistance, withdrawal from treatment, or even a suicide attempt.

In the treatment of the perverse patient, the dynamics of transference offer particularly potent "therapeutic leverage" for the analyst. The potential effectiveness of direct prohibition of perverse behavior was indicated by Dr. Ostow's comment with respect to a particular case: "Not only did the analyst become associated with the superego but, because there was a libidinal character to the relationship and because obedience is the expression of libidinal desire, he was obeyed by the patient." Since both the primary focus of the analysis and its most intractable locus of resistance is the area of the patient's earliest object relations, the analyst must pay persistent attention to those themes and their constantly varied expressions in the transference. Often, the study group found, the transference stimulates homosexual acting-out that is so libidinized that it is difficult to indicate to the patient the distinction between fantasy and reality with respect to the analyst.

Positive transference leading to a negative therapeutic response was encountered in Case II. A male homosexual—reacting to the analyst's suggestion that he recognize and express his rage toward his mother—initiated a homosexual relationship. In this connection, Dr. Arlow commented: "It would seem that the patient was pursuing the omnipotent magical penis and hoped to get it from the male analyst. The analyst, in effect, turned the patient's wishes from castrating the powerful man to hating the woman, and the patient used this hatred of the woman for his defensive purposes. But leaving the analysis in a state of unresolved transference, he proceeded to act out.

"I am suggesting not only that a change in superego functioning triggered the homosexual acting-out at that particular point, but also that the intensification of the drive resulted from the transference situation. When the derivatives of the transference are not brought to the surface and discussed, some action often takes place.

With the breakup of the analysis, this defensive acting-out became consolidated in continuing homosexual activity. Ordinarily, if the analysis is going well and the transference aspects are analyzed, the tendency toward acting-out is less rather than greater."

Another kind of transference difficulty appeared in a case considered by the group where, as Dr. Sterba observed, perverse behavior was a manifestation of withdrawal and an expression of "revenge" against the analyst (Case I). Here, the patient's visits to prostitutes—which earlier had been eliminated during the course of analysis—were resumed even though the analyst was not absent. This behavior was seen as a compound act of revenge, solace-seeking, and self-rejection. It was, in Dr. Sterba's view, precipitated by the intensity of the transference relation in combination with the analyst's insistence (which the patient viewed as a rejection) on examining the realities of the marital relation. Dr. Furst thought that the patient had responded to an apparent rejection by the analyst—turning to another source of gratification was his established pattern for discharging libido when experiencing rejection. One often found, Dr. Sterba added, that the patient engaged in this type of "revenge" behavior when forced to continue working at an object relation which was difficult and unpleasant.

While in this case pregenital etiological factors were clearly indicated, the chief conflict was essentially oedipal: the patient, who believed that he was responding to his wife's "hateful" qualities, had to recognize that his behavior was channeled by his own oedipal guilt. The guilt was the primary source of inhibition in the particular marital relation, but had been masked by complaints against the spouse.

Fairly predictably, a patient may attempt to seek revenge or to "spite" through the resumption of perverse behavior when the analyst is absent. The reassertion of perverse behavior in this situation is facilitated by its utility in alleviating separation anxiety. In general, the suspension of analytic surveillance makes the resumption of the explicit perverse pattern even more enticing. Consider the following striking example: A patient traveled to the same city in which his analyst was attending a professional meeting because of which several of the patient's sessions had been cancelled. There he arranged for the company of prostitutes during his stay. An interesting aspect was that the cost of the prostitutes precisely matched the analyst's fees, had the appointments not been cancelled.

When the analyst attempts to compel the patient to face basically inconsistent attitudes and needs—in effect, to consider the ultimate consequences of removal from reality—it is sometimes possible to obtain his cooperation.* As Dr. Blos and Dr. Ostow asserted, to the degree that the transference provides gratification by recreating the original relation with the mother, the derivatives of the need can be decathected and "defused."

However, the group concurred that the special and interrelated dynamic elements found in the perverse personality—ranging from an extraordinary tolerance for inconsistency and an ego syntonic and conflict-free adaptation to the Oedipus conflict—make therapeutic intervention extraordinarily intricate and challenging.

The importance and complexity of constitutional components or predispositions and their implications for therapy were stressed by Dr. Valenstein:

> It is uncertain, at this point, whether the biologically impelled aspects of libidinal development vary from person to person and also whether such factors as oral or anal gratification are more heightened for some than for others. These questions were touched on in discussing eidetic imagery, the perceptual and the motor systems, and it appears that the givens—in terms of instinctual-ego reciprocity for some persons—vary from a very early stage, just as there are active children and quiescent children.

> That was, to a certain extent, Freud's position when he took a very broad and tolerant view of libidinal organization. He did not establish as a treatment goal the elimination of a perversion; rather, he wished to make it sufficiently ego and socially syntonic, insofar as it is possible within the society, that the patient may live a relatively mature life with respect to his capacity to work and to love on his own terms.

> Freud's treatment goals always remained particularly influenced by his notion of neurosogenesis and the origins of psychoanalytical theory and technique. Implicitly, if not explicitly, his position was that the analytic method is directed to those phases of

*The group noted that where a direct confrontation approach—a strict prohibition—produces suicidal threats or withdrawal from treatment as a "last line" defense, a deeper and more unpredictable pathology may be present.

development that follow verbalization and a definitive structuring of the person's psychic apparatus. It does not really have any efficacy—or even justification, in terms of its methodology—for those conditions that antedate the stage of verbalization and the development of intrapsychic conflict. ·

With respect to treatment, Dr. Valenstein said that if the defensive function of the perversion becomes relatively "uneconomical"—that is, if too much anxiety is generated by the behavior for the gratification that it provides—the exercise of the perversion may be impeded. That this functional decision is sometimes made by the individual is reflected in those patients whose perverse impulses remained at a latent level and are expressed and disguised in a reciprocal symptom.

As Dr. Kanzer noted, an oscillation of behavior frequently occurs between "a passive, childhood-related experience with a strong masochistic flavor and an active, often sadistic, solution based on identification with the original aggressor." A pattern of ambivalent alternation between passive masochism and active sadism was particularly evident in one patient who "signaled" her phasic identifications by both manner and dress. In the masochistic mode, she showed meekness and compliance and adopted exceedingly feminine attire; after having been exposed to "phallic slights" or penetration by her husband, she chose masculine dress and barely contained an aggressive, raging fury. In the sadistic phase of this cycle, the patient severely beat her young son.

In such cases, commented Dr. Valenstein, the "instinctualized defense lies in the masochism that is manifest. The objective must be constantly to present the patient with the evidence of the latent sadism. The patient gives the analyst only 'half of the grapefruit'—the masochism—and wants to be relieved of 'all this suffering.' He must be shown the other half of the grapefruit—the sadism—which was always implicit and has to be made explicit."

Optimally, the analytic exposure of the genesis of the perversion reduces the intensity of the craving and permits the interposition of a corrective perception. Analytic surveillance may cause the otherwise "unchallenged" patient to respond—through the intensification if not the generation of conflict—to feelings of shame and guilt, thus depriving him of the equilibrium state which he had achieved and its rationalization.

Perversion is more likely to respond to psychoanalytic treatment if there is a conscious rejection of the perverse tendency if, in Dr. Sterba's phrase, there is "sufficient inner drive to reintegration," and if defensive components outweigh libidinal components in the structuring of perverse acts. The more the perversion provides direct libidinal gratification and the less it is utilized for defense, the more it will resist treatment.

Overall, the best prognosis can be expected in those patients who reject their own perverse impulses; who do not achieve relief from conflict and anxiety by the behavior; who do not easily tolerate inconsistency in thought or practice; and who use the perversion primarily for defensive purposes.

For the analyst, the concomitant objectives are: (1) to expose the unconscious wish and denial behind the perversion; (2) to reinforce any superego strength in the effort to eliminate the behavior; and (3) through a modification of the oedipal relation in the transference, to facilitate in the patient a restructuring of the drives toward perversion. Essentially, the analytic aim is to achieve a sense of genital reality.

PART TWO
Cases

CASE I

A.B.,* a thirty-two-year-old man, has been in analysis for about eight months. He came for help because he was having serious problems in his marriage; he felt he had repeated in his present marriage much of what had gone on between his parents.

When the patient entered analysis initially, he complained that he was unable to achieve close human relationships, particularly with women, and he deeply wished to establish more satisfying relationships in his life. He did not say that he was unable to have sexual relations with women; in fact, he boasted of an extremely active sexual life. However, in addition to his difficulty in establishing meaningful relationships, he felt that he never belonged to the "in group" in any situation, and that he could not accomplish much. He recognized he had many abilities, but always felt that he was never able to use them effectively or to be aggressive

*These initials are assigned to each case in alphabetical order. They bear no necessary relation to the name of the patient, which was not revealed to the group. Where significant data are missing, they have been omitted to protect the privacy of the patient.

enough. Above all, he claimed, he wanted to achieve marriage, home, and children.

The patient did not mention his perversion for many months. He glamorized his sexual life, made vague allusions to "wild sex," and revealed the details of his perversion only very gradually.

The patient was rather short—five feet four inches tall—and this fact played a large role in his fantasy life. He felt that his height was a factor in his feeling disadvantaged.

The patient was an only child in a lower-middle-class Jewish family. According to his descriptions, his mother was very strict and domineering, compulsive about the household and about organizing activities on schedule. She imposed the same perfectionism on her son. He remembered being kept immaculate as an infant; his mother changed him constantly so that he was always dry. The patient was musically talented and became a violinist, following in the footsteps of other members of the family who were distinguished violinists. His mother demanded that he practice many hours a day, and, as an obedient child, he did so.

At some point in latency he resisted to the extent of insisting that he stop his musical education, and his mother finally yielded. When he was a young man, the hostility between the patient and his mother was intense. His mother would become furious with him, and the patient fantasied that she might lose control in her anger. However, when they learned that she had become ill, his attitude changed completely; he became very loving and tender and wished that he might marry in order to give his mother a grandchild. He was quite sad after her death.

The patient's father was highly moral and well respected in his field. The patient, who described his father as prissy, exacting and precise, felt that he never had his father's full support; that his father, like his mother, demanded too much of him. He cited, as an example of his father's attitude toward him, that he always felt that his father was rooting for his opponent. The analyst felt there may have been some truth to this perception.

The patient had been graduated from college and obtained a position with a large concern in New York City. He had been successful and had become a junior executive, but felt that he would never achieve a senior position in the firm because he was Jewish, and this perception, too, may have been accurate. Nevertheless, he enjoyed the junior position. It was at this point that the analysis began.

The patient's acting-out of perverse behavior had started when he was in his twenties. The analyst knew that the behavior followed the death of the mother, but the patient never made a direct connection between the two events. The analyst cited a fantasy the patient had, after his mother's death, about eating his mother's body, which the analyst considered a symptom of separation anxiety. He emphasized to the study group, however, that his conjecture about a connection between the death of the mother and the triggering of the perverse behavior was just a hunch.

On the surface, the perversion itself was highly masochistic. The patient sought prostitutes and explored their attitudes by asking them, for example, "What is the worst thing you have ever done with a man?" He was clever and subtle about getting a prostitute to reveal any perverse tendencies she might have. His own aim was to get the prostitute to perform some humiliating act upon him. Ideally, he preferred to lie on the floor or in the bathtub and have the prostitute walk over him and urinate on him. Short of that, he required her to crouch over him with his face pressed against her genital area, and to have her push on his head and command him, in a very domineering manner, to perform cunnilingus on her.

As time went on, he began to demand more and more humiliating acts. He particularly liked to have another prostitute present to observe his degradation. The women had to show contempt, amusement, and enjoyment of his plight before he became excited. After the humiliation had been completed to his satisfaction and he was sufficiently aroused, the patient would perform a conventional act of intercourse. If, at the same time, the prostitute described humiliations she planned for the next time, his excitement would be heightened. After an experience of this kind, the orgasm would give him a sense of total relief. In the analysis, he would act out the sense of relief on the couch, feeling drained, but not depressed.

Interestingly, although he had many fantasies of being defecated on, the conscious idea was too repugnant for him to act it out in reality. He imposed other limits on the situations he created for himself: For example, on one occasion a prostitute was intensely excited by this game and began to be genuinely domineering. She forced his head into her genital area so hard that he became uncomfortable. He stopped then, and said, "Look here, who's paying?"

He rarely returned to the same prostitute, and in the course of the analysis it became clear that one aspect of his game of humiliation was the need to control the situation. He was intensely afraid that a prostitute might humiliate him in circumstances he had not designed himself. The same fear prevented him from acting out his perversion when he went to brothels with other men, as he often did.

The analyst then turned to the subject of the patient's fantasy life, which began in childhood and was very rich. The analyst learned only recently that the patient started masturbating when he was about six years old and continued to do so frequently up to the present time. The patient's childhood fantasies were all connected in some way with anal activities. He imagined being tied underneath a horse and looking up into the horse's anus. Another fantasy, which began when he was about eight years old, was derived from reading stories about the Puritans in stocks. In the fantasy, he would be locked in the stocks and people would throw things at him, particularly horse feces. The fecal aspect of the fantasy excited him most.

The patient remembered being aroused by the thought of the greased wagon wheel on the old beer trucks. At about the same time, he constructed a fantasy in which he was in the bottom of an outhouse looking up while a queen was defecating. He also remembered masturbating anally by putting a little toy soldier into his rectum, taking it out, and smelling it. When he was about ten years old, he was intensely interested in a girl cousin. They went into a bathroom to examine each other, and he first reported the sight as mildly repugnant. Later on in the analysis, this first report was altered. (See Chapter II.)

When the patient was about thirteen years old, he and an older boy visited together a young woman with whom he thought they had intercourse. He cannot recall this experience exactly now. But he remembered being shocked. The patient had no further sexual relations until he was in his early twenties. He remembered going out with girls when he was in high school and petting, but he disliked kissing. He was not interested in affectionate relations with girls, although he knew other people felt differently. In talking about his sexual experiences, the patient reported that he constantly tried to get himself in a position where his face would be close to a girl's buttocks. These actions were always stealthy, and he kept a record of the number of women he managed to touch in this fashion.

The patient was also a voyeur when he was very young. He spent hours watching the windows of his neighbors, hoping to catch a glimpse of a woman. He believed that his father had an uncanny way of knowing when he was occupied in this fashion and was always able to walk into his room and interrupt him just as something interesting was about to happen.

When he was about twelve or thirteen, he turned to exhibitionism, again in a stealthy manner.

When he was eighteen or nineteen years old, he attempted to act out in a minor way the kind of thing he did overtly with prostitutes later on: He would suggest that a girl allow him to put his face near the genital area. Once, the girl to whom he made the suggestion said she would allow it the next time he took her out, but he never took her out again; apparently the impulse both attracted and terrified him.

During his college days the patient was in military service. Although he encountered many opportunities for sexual experimentation, he was too frightened of venereal disease to explore them.

He began going out with prostitutes when he was in his early twenties. Then, having become more aggressive, he began going out with other women, particularly "wild girls," as he described them. He preferred married women, and these affairs followed the same pattern as his relationships with prostitutes in that, if he was successful in persuading a woman to have a sexual relationship with him, he never saw her again.

Before he began analysis, he had had only one relationship that lasted for several months. He grew very uncomfortable in it and discontinued seeing the girl without explanation. The analyst had the impression that the sexual relationship, in this instance, was relatively free of perversion.

When he entered analysis, the patient felt that his whole life had been a masochistic existence. His feelings of being disadvantaged were associated with his height, his Jewishness, domination by his mother, the rigid training he had undergone and his mother's overprotectiveness. In the early months of his analysis, he began to realize that much of this feeling was self-imposed, that he could have made friends, but had always elected to turn down the opportunity. He set up situations that he could interpret to himself as experiences of rejection.

His reference to repeating, in his marriage, much of what went on between his parents was connected with his fantasy that his parents never had any sexual relations. He remembered that in his early years his parents spent evenings at home reading, but never had any contact the patient could imagine as sexual. The current situation between him and his wife was similar; she was resistant to sexual relations and he was not eager for them.

He felt that the perverse tendencies were beginning to govern his entire sexual life. He felt driven to more and more humiliating practices with prostitutes and was afraid that eventually he might be able to have intercourse only through these means.

As the analysis progressed, the patient began to complain that he had become a slave at home. After working all day, he would have to play with his children at night. Then he could not get any rest because, if one of the children had a slight cold, he would climb into bed with his father and the patient could not sleep.

At this point in the presentation, the study group members proposed some preliminary formulations: (1) since a humiliation requirement appears commonly in female masochists, in this case it suggested feminine identification; (2) fixation was established by the mother's heavy pressures during toilet training; (3) the perversion may have represented a rebirth fantasy; (4) the sexual fantasies remained the patient's only secret, private domain; (5) the form of the perversion suggested hostility to the mother and provocation of hostility from her back to the patient; (6) the perversion established a regression to a cloacal theory; (7) the perversion was established by the mother's allowing the patient to share the toilet with her; (8) watching for the fecal penis relieved the patient's castration anxiety; (9) preoccupation with the female perineum represented the wish to return to the mother's body and may have led to claustrophobic and entrapment fantasies.

The analyst pointed out, with reference to the humiliation scenes with prostitutes, that having himself been humiliated gave the patient the right to be aggressive in return and to have sexual relations with a woman.

At the next meeting of the study group, the members suggested that the pattern of humiliation with the prostitute represented the converse of the sadistic, aggressive attitude toward the mother. The question of the use of the aggressive and sexual drives was discussed. One member of the study group suggested that, when the anger of the child against the mother turned against the self in a masochistic perversion, the object of the hatred became the object of the love as well. The fusion, the erotization of the aggression, was conditioned by the fact that both were the same object. Another member of the study group elaborated this theme, pointing out that the adaptive goal, the biologic goal of the masochistic perversion, is intended through a wearing away process to reverse itself and provide a happy ending. The original traumatic event, whether erotic or otherwise, is repeated with the idea that it can be undone, controlled, and mastered.

The analyst then resumed his account of the case. He reported that the patient himself raised a question the analyst had wondered about: "I can see that my desires, my wishes, are as far out as homosexual wishes; why didn't I become a homosexual?" The analyst felt that the reason was that his object was the mother; his battle with his drive was his battle with his mother, and even the prostitute symbolized a degraded mother. He was trying to solve his oedipal problem and had a tremendous amount of guilt over his aggressiveness. Even in the act of perversion, he was overwhelmed with guilt because it represented revenge upon his mother. The analyst saw the same dynamics in the transference—in acting-out with a prostitute, he revenged himself on the analyst. A few months earlier, the analyst had to attend a meeting in San Francisco and missed four sessions with the patient. Having been warned about this in advance, the patient engaged two prostitutes in San Francisco; this arrangement cost him the same amount of money as the four sessions.

The patient developed a fantasy in which a prostitute watched him intently as he put his face in her perineum. The magic lay in the knowledge that she was the observer. He saw that this fantasy involved a repetition, although he had no conscious memory of anything in his childhood that would connect directly with it. The previous summer the patient had been invited to join a married couple who had a reputation for sexual experimentation. He accepted the invitation and had sexual relations with the wife while the husband watched and kissed his wife on the forehead as the patient was having intercourse with her. He found the situation very gratifying and he was very potent in it. Although this acting-out involved no anal contact, in his fantasies he always turned to the anal region. Earlier in the course of the analysis, he recognized that the prostitute did not exist for him as a person; only the anogenital area existed.

The analyst suggested that the patient's resolution of his problem with aggression and guilt was of decisive importance—he recognized and was terrified of his feelings of rage. When he read about a murder trial involving a professional murderer, he felt he could have been such a murderer and expressed wildly sadistic fantasies about ripping a woman apart with a penis and smashing in her face. He equated the relief that he felt from acting-out with a prostitute to the relief he obtained when, feeling sure that he was in the right, he reprimanded another person without feeling guilt, in a nonsexual situation. Although, on the surface, his experiences with prostitutes were masochistic, these nonsexual situations in which he was able to express anger without guilt seemed to be sadistic. However, the contradiction was misleading; the analyst thought that defusion of the instincts was involved here. The situation with a prostitute was both sadistic and masochistic in that, after the patient had been humiliated, the alleviation of guilt permitted him to do anything he wanted. Although he did not act out sadistic behavior with a prostitute, during intercourse, he had fantasies of humiliating her. The patient, then, could be more extravagant in the passive act, in terms of perversion, than he could in the active sadistic role; and he himself said that he could be aggressive, even in his dreams.

Gradually, the patient was able to inhibit the practice of the perversion. Formerly he had visited prostitutes frequently; now he did so rarely, usually during vacations. On these occasions he had feelings of guilt and shame about the behavior; he had become aware that it was shoddy, shabby; he no longer glamorized the prostitutes. Whenever he was unable to inhibit the impulse success-fully, he avoided the analytic session for at least two days. On these occasions the analyst felt that the patient was unable to face him because the acting-out episode was an expression of anger and spite and revenge. The patient was consciously aware that his life tendency was to become angry, and then to fail. Among the fan-tasies he had of failing in the analysis was that he would be cured, and then his penis would be cut off.

As he gained insight into his rationalizations for his behavior, he became more unhappy than he had ever been. He no longer found as much pleasure in the perversion; he went to a prostitute only when he felt tension building to an intolerable degree. In the past, he had no problems with sleep, but now he was occasionally insomniac. He tried to manage the tension in various ways, such as taking walks and masturbating.

His sexual life with his wife was nonexistent at this point.

Recently, primal-scene material has been appearing. For example, the patient dreamed that he and his wife were in an automobile and that a man came over and "operated," kissed his wife and asked for a date. The patient was hoping that she would refuse. A fragment from the same dream concerned an older woman who possessed a laser beam. The analyst interpreted it as repetition of some primal-scene observation. The patient tended to become more anxious whenever this interpretation was presented, and his reaction to the anxiety was an impulse to seek out a prostitute again.

Many of his dreams were nightmares in which women were pursuing and clutching him; in one, the woman was a crippled girl, with one leg shorter than the other, who beckoned to him with claw-like hands. Another dream was concerned with degradation. A car appeared driven by himself or someone else who had the same first name. The car had to be turned around in a horseshoe drive (a reference to horse manure) and it was necessary to back over a newly planted lawn which was wet and soft. The car, a brown Rolls-Royce, ploughed through the lawn twice and ruined it; the patient was left helplessly yelling after the driver to stop. The patient recognized the many references to anal material—the brown Rolls-Royce, the mud on the lawn, the terrible mess of the situation—and then he recognized that the driver was himself and that the dream was about his own aggressivness and his feeling of wanting to make a mess of everything. At the same time, he also recognized that here again was a suggestion of three people: another man, a woman, and himself.

In another dream, the patient sat down in a dental chair. The dentist got a grip on a tooth and said, "Now I've got a good grip on you." The patient shouted, "All watch lights out! All watch lights out!" Then a woman distracted the dentist by screaming and he lost his grip. The patient recognized that the dentist was the analyst and that the dream was concerned with both his castration anxiety and primal-scene material, and the tremendous anxiety connected with them.

A member of the study group suggested that these almost nightmarish preoccupations with the witchlike, Lady Macbeth women indicated that the patient saw the female genital as a castrating horror which would attract and snare him. He therefore regressed to a pregenital anal sadism as a defense. The analyst agreed with this interpretation because he too had the impression that the patient had progressed to genitality and that his perversion was a regressive phenomenon rather than a persistence of a very early anal fixation. He pointed out that the dreams also had an almost literal vagina-dentata fantasy quality; particularly the dream about the dentist. The analyst reported that the patient's considerable problem with guilt showed in a variety of ways. He had a fantasy that one drop of urine somehow entered his stomach and had poisoned him. This fantasy was in turn related to his mother, who died of accidental poisoning.

The analyst then summarized the chief themes that had appeared in the analysis since the previous meeting of the group: The analysis had spoiled all the patient's fun; it was a repetition of the rigid schedule of practicing the violin that had so infuriated him in his childhood. Another theme was his angry reaction to the feeling of being neglected because of his wife's derelictions. Not only was she sexually rejecting, but he considered her a rather sloppy person. Despite the patient's perverse wish to be degraded in his own fashion, he couldn't tolerate sloppiness. He had also recognized that his urge to fail represented his wish to revenge himself on his mother and that his perverse activities with prostitutes were a lesser evil in that they protected him from failing in his work. But he also recognized that the retreat to the prostitute had become impossible because it threatened his marriage.

The patient, then, was relatively unhappy and slightly depressed because the *analyst's supervision* had deprived him of the solutions he had sought in perversion. Now he had no solution, although he was striving toward one. He felt that his wife was a suitable partner and he did make efforts to establish a better relationship with her, but he could not sustain these because he became terrified of her rejection.

At the next meeting of the study group, the members focused on the issue of the patient's anxiety. The analyst believed that the perversion served to overcome anxiety, and cited a report by the patient about an occasion when he was very anxious and responded to the anxiety by going to a prostitute. When he had the prostitute urinate over him, he looked very carefully at her genital area and thought he saw a little penis there. In talking about it, he had the fantasy of biting off this crayon-like penis. He was vague as to whether it was in the vaginal, the perineal, or the anal area.

In an extended discussion about the meaning of having a prostitute urinate on him, the group hypothesized that, in addition to its defensive and anxiety-binding function, this behavior also served as an expression of the patient's excitement aroused by bedwetting in childhood. The analyst told the group that the patient had been unable to remember any enuretic problems, although at one time the analyst had reconstructed an episode of enuresis from a dream, which the patient confirmed in part. The analyst inferred that the patient's linking of urination and sexual excitement has been elaborated to the cloacal theory. The patient consciously remembered that his concept of female anatomy was that there was one hole which served both for urination and defecation, and in front of the woman was a hairy place without a penis.

The analyst then summarized what had occurred in the analysis during the previous month. "The patient was encouraged for the first several weeks about what had been happening within himself, feeling that he was becoming more overtly aggressive and closer to his wife. Then the material switched and changed, partly in response to the patient's bringing up primal-scene dream material and his anxiety about what happens during intercourse. This shift was reflected in a deterioration in his relationship with his wife. In the same circular pattern, he became more critical of her; as she responded by becoming colder, he developed more anxiety about the relationship; he dealt with the anxiety by visiting a prostitute, and then developed even greater anxiety."

At this point, the patient again shifted and tried to be more tender with his wife because he thought that she might be considering divorce. In a fairly recent hour, the patient opened the session by detailing a long dream. In the dream, he paddled a rubber life raft about fifty feet across very rough water to an island, where there was a disreputable inn. The owner of the inn told the dreamer that it was much too dangerous to come across in the life raft and that he needed a better boat in which to go back. He pointed out an oddly shaped lifeboat and said, "That's a good one to go in if you're just divorced." The boat was a cabin cruiser, but the cabin was aft and sloped downward to the stern.

The scene changed; the patient was on some street on which there was an old Cadillac with Georgia license plates. He heard that a "rumble" was about to take place. He and a friend drove to a bar in order to be safe. The bar, or restaurant, had various levels. On the lower levels were a restaurant and a clean kitchen in which he saw an attractive girl. The scene changed again and the dreamer was in a dive in which there were many prostitutes. As the owner told him to take any girl he chose, the dream ended.

The patient's associations to the dream were many: He thought it was good that he faced danger in the dream by paddling on the rubber raft; he thought that looking into the various levels of the strange bar was a reference to the analysis in which he looked into the deeper levels of himself; he associated the cabin with the vagina, because it was plush on the inside.

The patient recalled that he had been rather irritable lately and seemed to be itching for a fight. He then talked of an attractive stewardess he knew, who is taller than he; he countered this with the thought that he really had other things in his favor to offset his short stature.

Later in the hour, he referred to the rubber dinghy as a survival life raft, the kind used in the navy.

The patient spoke about his physical cowardice, of which he was ashamed. He was frightened by the possibility of divorce. His wish to maintain the marriage was based partly on his feelings of guilt toward his wife.

The analyst interpreted the dream as an allegorical representation of the patient's feelings about sexual relations. The boat was a vagina; the reference to water was a reference to the urinary aspects of his sexual desires; he wanted a safe vagina, one that was white and clean.

The patient himself was troubled by what he conceived of as violent aspects to sexual relations and all the dangers implicit in the dream. He admitted toward the end of the hour that he was consciously aware of his fear of the vagina. He said that his wife seemed to change into something like a werewolf when they were in bed. The affect in the first part of the dream was mild anxiety, followed by great pleasure that he had faced the danger and paddled across the dangerous water. The rumor of a rumble provoked anxiety.

The analyst suggested that, when the patient could experience conflict in terms of drive representation, he externalized it and masked the conflict in concrete action. This was the ego aspect of his perversion. He felt that by the action itself, he resolved the conflict; he could consider himself a man when he had faced all the dangers involved in going to prostitutes. Formerly, he had described his perverse behavior as taking terrible chances and claimed he was proud of himself for doing so. At this point in the analysis, he was no longer so proud.

A member of the study group suggested that the mother's attitude toward toilet training and bathroom habits implied disgust, punitiveness, and interest, simultaneously. Consequently, the patient became fixed on this complex. Nevertheless he did progress further, developing oedipal and genital interests, which were so threatening and forbidding that he regressed to the position of fixation, which became the basis of his perversion.

The analyst summarized the material to date. He said that his own impression of his patient was that there was a strong regressive tendency operating in his problem. He pointed out that the patient attempted to establish some kind of object relation, even with prostitutes, and offered a recent example that also illuminated the patient's relationship to the analyst.

The patient arrived five minutes late for his appointment and thought the analyst was looking at him as though he was in resistance. When asked what he himself thought, he agreed that he was in resistance because he had had a contact the night before. He had met a girl who was interested in women as well as men. He told her about his experience with the married couple in which the husband had been the voyeur while the patient had intercourse with the wife. The wife, too, was interested in women. The patient invited the girl to come to his office to call the woman and verify the story. The girl was on one phone, the patient on an extension. The other woman began talking about her perverse activities and the patient became very excited. He put down the phone and rushed to the girl in his office because he wanted to perform cunnilingus on her while she was talking on the telephone. She was not interested, but afterward she said, "Drop something in the pocketbook and we can proceed." He described her as shy because she undressed only to her slip. This, the analyst felt, was a repetition of the mother situation. When he started performing cunnilingus on the girl, he looked up and saw that she was smiling. Then he tickled her perineum with his tongue. They both lay on the floor and he began talking to her about the next time they were going to meet and exciting her with stories about the other woman. At this point he became sufficiently excited to be able to penetrate.

The incident illustrated the patient's need to establish some kind of relationship, to elicit the cooperation and enjoyment of his partner; it was the partner's arousal that excited him sufficiently to have intercourse, but the experience of coitus itself was of less importance to him. In fact, he said coital sensation was somewhat blunted. In a sense, the patient was attempting to anesthetize the superego. However, the analyst pointed out, the anesthetic quality of the intercourse—the inhibition—occurred in this particular act because the girl was not interested in acting out the urination fantasy. The analyst continued: "When you looked into the perversion, you saw a tremendous amount of condensation. The first was that the female must enter into a kind of childish game. The tendency to play games might be considered an ego characteristic which facilitated perverse behavior, but the game itself also had a regressive quality—it was like small children playing in the bathroom, not real people doing anything dangerous. It was a mischievous act aimed against the parents, without the parents' knowledge." This was one of the problems the patient had in analysis; talking about the perversion meant letting the parent know about it.

The analyst saw the urination game as a defense against castration anxiety, against the terrible fear the patient had of the penisless woman. The patient was terrified of being sexually assertive. He was able to be aggressive only against his wife, and then only verbally; he could not be aggressive sexually. Much of the patient's fear derived from his conception of the vagina as a terrifying object. Curiously, he still did not have accurate knowledge of a woman's genital anatomy.

The study group opened the next session with a summary of the material presented at the previous meeting. They suggested that the patient's aggression probably had multiple causes: (1) the realistic temptation and frustration by the mother on both the oral and the anal levels during childhood; (2) anger at the object resulting from the object's compliance with the patient's desire to be degraded; (3) a need to express aggression through ego function; and (4) a drive to act out rather than to imagine.

The analyst reported that the patient's behavior pattern with prostitutes had changed; he visited them even while seeing the analyst regularly. On one such visit when he and the prostitute started to drive to an apartment, his teeth were chattering and his body was shaking so violently that he could barely put the key into the ignition. Yet, although the transaction contained all the elements that usually gave him such a sense of release, this time the sense of release was missing. The analyst thought that the patient was acknowledging indirectly that the analysis had interfered, to some degree, with his perverse behavior.

Later on the patient mentioned a newspaper story about a pervert who had been arrested, examined psychiatrically, and sent to jail. The examinations indicated that the man was dangerous because there was an aggressive element in his perverse behavior with children. After being sentenced to jail, the man in the case said he was treated unfairly. This reaction was much the way the patient felt—that somehow things are always unfair to him.

In subsequent hours, the analyst returned to the incident in which the patient visited the prostitute and elicited another element about which the patient found it very difficult to report; namely, that he had been thoroughly humiliated by the prostitute before the whole act began. The day after this acknowledgment, the patient reported a dream. "I dreamt my physician's son telephoned me and told me that he (the physician) had died."

The analyst suggested to the group that, as the patient's problems with aggression had begun to emerge, his well-defended perverse behavior had begun to lose some of its function. He thought that the aggressive wishes were interfering with the patient's relationship with his wife; that he still conceived of sexual relations as a murderous procedure.

The analyst also commented about superego permission in the development of the patient's perverse behavior and suggested that the mother had encouraged or at least permitted perverse behavior in the patient's childhood. The analyst was now inclined to think that the one healthy element in the patient's early development was that his father was not aligned with this type of behavior. Thus the analyst, as the physician-father, represented the person who safeguarded him. The patient was not sure that he could really give up the perversion, but he felt that the analyst opposed it.

The patient agreed that the dream said that the analyst was like the father who interfered with the boy's voyeuristic activity. In the dream itself, when the patient received the telephone message he reacted first with shock and then with dismay; tears welled up in his eyes. The analyst considered this reaction part of his ambivalence toward the analyst-father who, he hoped, would rescue him, but who also interfered with his perverse pleasure.

Since being genuinely humiliated by the prostitute, the patient had been seeking other prostitutes, some even more expensive than the one who had degraded him. Nevertheless, he had not been able to achieve pleasure in these activities, so he was forced to face some of his anxieties about proper sexual relationship with his wife.

A member of the study group pointed out that the patient had divided the maternal image into two: the idealized mother who remained the mother, and the degraded mother who became the wife.

The main task of the analysis was to work through the patient's defense, which consisted of making a game of almost every situation and never accepting full responsibility for his actions. This was not only true of his behavior with prostitutes but also with his wife. His attitudes, actions, and attacks—even though they were sexualized—were intentionally histrionic, because he wished to create a feeling of guilt. He even attempted to create this feeling in the analysis. For example, when the analyst was a few minutes late one morning, the patient said, "You were late. I always get here a few minutes before time. Why do you have to be late? You can't give this time back to me, even though you extend the hour so that I get the fifty minutes. Still, this is time that has been lost for me and you can never give it back." In other words: "You have to feel guilty."

The analyst believes that the patient attempted to make the analyst feel guilty as a way of defending himself against his own anxieties and guilt. The patient was just beginning to appreciate the intensity of his guilt feelings, particularly in terms of his perversion, but he didn't know whether he would be able to give up the defense. He saw that the guilt-eliciting aspect of the game was a replication of his mother's behavior with him. If he did not practice the violin, she would say, "Look how much you have hurt me by not practicing, by not using your talent." His mother had many techniques for making him feel guilty and he is beginning to see that his own behavior was aimed at creating a feeling of guilt in someone else.

The analyst reported that the patient had become somewhat aware of the homosexual aspect of the transference. He reported a dream in which he walked into a detective agency office and a man said to him, "Do you want someone who will kiss?" The patient declined, and the man then said, "Do you want someone who will piss?" The dream, the analyst inferred, indicated that the homosexual transference was beginning. He suggested that the patient retreated from the oedipal position because of his almost overwhelming fear of an oedipal type of love. The fear sent him into reverse, and his perversion prevented him from being homosexual. In the dream about the detective agency, for example, he said, "I'm glad I'm a pervert and not a homosexual." In other words, if he weren't a pervert he would be a homosexual. Caught in this dilemma, he had to hold onto both the analysis and the perversion; both protected him from the homosexuality.

A member of the study group suggested that the patient really felt that certain people ought to feel guilty, particularly the mother and father figures, and that primal-scene material was emerging. The analyst agreed with this formulation and mentioned that the question of primal-scene material arose about seven months previous to this report.

He has struggled against a real transference neurosis and is beginning to give himself to the analysis now that some of his defenses—particularly the game aspect of his behavior—have been punctured.

The study group suggested several formulations: (1) Anxiety had appeared in recent perverse episodes and was implied by other phenomena, such as loss of sexual gratification. (2) The patient's return to the prostitute represented revenge against the analyst for encouraging his reunion with his wife. (3) The perverse behavior failed to give satisfaction because it represented revenge and was the acting-out of the homosexual relation to the analyst. (4) The patient concealed and minimized his sadism in the perversion by play-acting. (5) The emerging homosexual transference to the analyst affected the patient's behavior in his sessions and may have contributed to his anxiety. (6) The prostitute's control over the situation destroyed the defensive system which protected him against castration anxiety and guilt, through perversion. (7) The patient experienced óedipal anxiety in the form of phobias as a result of feeling coerced into strengthening his relation with his wife. The perverse activity with a prostitute represented a playful satisfaction of these oedipal desires, free from the anxiety a real relationship would engender. (8) The patient did not always distinguish clearly between game playing and reality; his perversion was a game, but it was also real. This behavior was similar to that of some children who are unable to reconcile private reality with objective reality. (9) The perverse activity represented a flight from a strengthening of the homosexual transference relation.

The analyst told the group that he was glimpsing different parts of the dynamics and that the parts were beginning to present a coherent picture. He reported that the patient's perversion no longer offered satisfaction or relief; he expressed a great desire to return to the prostitute who humiliated him, yet he had not done so. He wanted to overcome the trauma of the failure, but was unable to make the attempt. He rationalized his retreat from the perversion on the grounds that relationships with prostitutes involved the risks of ruining his marriage and perhaps of contracting syphilis and becoming sterile.

The analyst reported that he and the patient had again discussed the recent incident in which he had become overwhelmed with anxiety while with a prostitute, but the patient had repressed his anxiety and claimed that what he experienced was not fear, but anticipation. Slowly, however, he was beginning to remember the anxiety.

Since the last group meeting the patient had only two extramarital experiences, both of them unsatisfactory. In the first, he and another man went to a massage parlor where the patient was masturbated by a woman. The analyst interpreted this device as a protection against both anxiety and the homosexual element. In the other incident, the patient, unable to hire a prostitute who was willing to perform the urinating act, accepted another girl and requested fellatio. In these experiences, the patient avoided inserting his penis into the vagina. He continued to insist that he had no fear of it, but within a few minutes, the material turned again to his terror of the vagina.

The analyst then discussed two of the patient's problems—anxiety about aggression and fear of intercourse.

The patient opened one session by asking himself whether he should permit his mind to go free, go wild, then remarked, "I would really like to blast or yell at my employees." He turned to the problem of his imagining his wife as a werewolf at night.

The patient was exceedingly anxious about any aggressive act he undertook. He had a constant feeling that something terrible was going to happen to him and he wondered whether this feeling had anything to do with his treatment of his wife. On the other hand, when he became angry with her, he felt that he had the right to go to a prostitute.

Thinking of his activities with prostitutes, he reverted to the idea that if the woman urinated on him and put something into him, he then had the right to put something into her.

In the interim, before the next session, the patient became very aware of resistance to the analysis. He did not want to come to the session, feeling that it was like practicing the violin. When he arrived for the session, he discussed his conflicting feelings about making a tentative date with a divorcée he knew. He really didn't want an affair: It would be dangerous; the information might get back to his wife; it might interfere with his marriage. The patient then reported a dream. He was in a car with a "wild" girl; and they drove to a suburban split-level house with a glass sliding door. The door led onto a lawn with the sidewalk at the outer edge. The door's handle swung out at a ninety-degree angle, with a hook-like arrangement to stop the swing. Strangely, the hook-like arrangement was at the bottom of the door, not at the middle or the top. The girl asked whether anyone could see into the house, because the curtains were sheer. He stepped out to see if it were possible and said no, but he did see two girls in the house. One had her hand on the other's crotch. The other pushed her away. Then the patient realized that the parents were home in the house across the street. The girl who had come with him protested that too much could be seen. The patient noticed a man outside, looking the other way. The girl then said that it would be all right to go to Rockaway. The dream ended.

The reference to Rockaway was connected with the patient's wife, who came from there originally. It had become a lower-class neighborhood, although it used to be primarily middle class. The patient did not grow up there. He compared the doors to shower doors. The patient was back in the bathroom of his sexuality. The door handle was peculiar in that it was built for a rod to go into: a curtain rod, for example, but a curtain rod would be at the top of the door and this was at the bottom.

The patient realized that the reference in the dream to curtains was a reference to peeking. He associated this as an anxiety that his father might catch him in the house in the dream. He wondered whether this might refer to his childhood idea that his father magically knew when to enter his room to catch him peeking into neighbors' windows.

At this point, the analyst interpreted the patient's associations, tracing some of his anxieties and the representation in the material of primal-scene experiences. He suggested that the peeking and the patient's fears and anxieties about the father's coming into the house represented, in reverse, an experience the patient had as a child.

A member of the study group suggested that one reason the perverse experience no longer provided relief for this patient was that the castration anxiety, which previously had applied only to his wife and idealized women, had been associated with the prostitutes. The patient now realized that the prostitutes, too, have female genitals.

The analyst agreed that the anxiety had indeed been extended, but also the patient's capacity to fantasy a penis inside the vagina had been failing. The patient used the fantasy to relieve his anxiety, but this primary problem—the fear of the female genital—had not been fully resolved.

The analyst felt that the patient's private world was being exposed. The patient reported a dream in which the analyst accused him of not telling everything and the patient asked, "What am I not telling you?" The analyst replied, "You don't tell me about the kosher language." Although the patient had no associations to this, the analyst thought the dream referred to the private language, the private life, the private reality in which he lived. The analyst also saw in the material he has presented the homosexual transference again emerging and interfering with all the patient's sources of sexual gratification except masturbation.

A member of the study group suggested that the perverse act itself served as a relief, a defense against anxiety rather than a source of anxiety. He considered the fear of the vagina represented the patient's guilt feeling in relation to the father: namely, that the object of the sex act was forbidden, and the act must incur punishment.

The analyst agreed with this observation and he reported a recent fantasy as an example of the patient's enormous guilt about his perversion. The fantasy was in the form of a story he told a woman in an attempt to find out whether she would be interested in a perverse act. He told her about an office manager who treated his women employees very strictly and sometimes cruelly. One day he came into the office intoxicated and passed out; the girls urinated on him in revenge. The act of urination represented aggression and degradation, but the patient displaced the aggression: it was really a man who urinated on another man as his dreams about wetting indicated. The patient must always disguise the aggressive element.

A member of the study group suggested two approaches to the matter of perversion. The first was the developmental theory, in which a literal experience of seduction and aggressivity, possibly at a preverbal or pregenital stage, created a fixation in the individual's sexuality. According to the second theory, as the perverse person developed and gained sophistication, conflict arose, particularly around oedipal scenes. Another member of the study group suggested that the therapeutic challenge in perversion was that the experientially focused, structured patterns of action for discharge may have been relatively autonomous, having been established before conflict entered and therefore fundamentally independent of conflict even when the conflict exploited the perverse discharge pattern.

A third member of the study group agreed that the perversion may have resulted from a fixation at an infantile level of development, in which case it was conflict-free; but he suggested that patients with perversions who entered analysis did so because the anxiety engendered by the need for genital adaptation was enormous.

The analyst felt that the patient had sacrificed a great deal in his analytic work. Although his perversion no longer offered him relief, a different satisfaction was sustaining him; namely, the feeling that the analyst was taking care of him.

A member of the study group made the final comment that an analyst treating a patient with perverse symptoms must open to discussion the factors that determined the patient's choice of action. The conflicts must be examined, regardless of the direction in which they took the patient and only if he himself elected to turn toward normal heterosexual behavior, did the analyst have the right to insist on this resolution as the therapeutic goal.

CASE II

C.D., a man about forty-two years old, sought treatment because of acute anxiety attacks. He has been in analysis with his current analyst for about three years and was previously in treatment with another analyst for two years. He originally entered analysis because of episodes he characterized as "breakdowns"—periods of intense anxiety which threw him into a state of utter helplessness. These attacks were always triggered by situations in which he felt unable to meet the requirements of an unusually demanding ego ideal or superego.

He suffered acute anxiety when he entered his father's business. Everyone expected that he would be as brilliant as his father, but the patient felt that he could not live up to this standard. He left his father's firm and industry and found employment in another large publishing firm in Boston. He was unable to tolerate the demands of the responsibility placed upon him—a pattern that persisted throughout his life—and the first breakdown occurred. The patient is a slender man of medium height and inconspicuous appearance. He dresses conservatively, in a style consistent with his socioeconomic status. There is nothing effeminate in his clothing or his mannerisms.

The patient comes from a distinguished family which was dominated by his mother, although his father was well known and highly respected. The father, who in the family situation seemed to be a more passive personality, died when the patient was an adult. His mother is still alive.

In the ongoing analysis, the patient presented very little childhood material. The analyst attempted to reconstruct his early background from the way he functioned in adult life. He was brought up by his mother and by governesses. He did not like to play with other boys because he was weak and scrawny.

The one incident from early childhood that the patient reported was sexual play with a sister, primarily mutual exploration. The patient was a shy, weak child, overprotected by and extremely dependent upon his mother.

The analyst recounted an episode that illustrates how the patient's superego operates. When the patient was in boarding school—he was fifteen or sixteen years old—his grades were mediocre. His father wrote to him that, while he recognized that his son was not doing badly, he thought that everyone should do his best; it was obvious that his son was not. The letter made such an impression on the patient that he began to work very seriously and obtained a straight A average. In college and in graduate school he continued his record of high achievement. In the course of the analysis, he often reverted to this period and compared his current performance with his level of functioning at that time. He believed that he never realized his full potential subsequently, and the analyst felt that he was probably correct.

He did not participate in competitive games at college because he was shy. However, he became an accomplished mountain climber, won wide recognition, and felt greatly reassured by this success.

The patient became aware of homosexual inclinations in puberty, although it was a subliminal awareness. He had started to masturbate and discovered that magazine pictures of muscle men excited him sexually. He would go up into the attic to masturbate and then hide the magazines. He tried unsuccessfully to stop masturbating. In any case for a short time he vacillated between interest in boys and interest in girls. He remembered one trip, during his college years, when he accompanied his father on a business trip. He looked at girlie magazines and became very excited. He went to nightclubs with his father, who indirectly encouraged him to go to a prostitute. However, the patient was not able to take that step.

By this time, the patient was in analysis with his first analyst. Shortly after the trip with his father, the patient met a bisexual man. He was living with a woman; nevertheless, he seduced the patient into his first homosexual experience. The man was extraordinarily intense, both physically and emotionally, and the patient was tremendously in love with him. He found many kinds of gratification in this homosexual experience. Together, the two young men created rather unusual variations in their sexual experimentation; for example, they practiced analingus and poured a little whisky into the anus to make it more palatable.

The patient's partner was really most engrossed with his work however, and sometimes broke dates with the patient in order to continue working. The patient could not tolerate his not being the most important object in his partner's life and terminated the affair. For a period thereafter, he was homosexually promiscuous, and occasionally became deeply involved in personal relationships, though none was as intense as that with his first partner.

The patient was about twenty-two or twenty-three years old when this first overt homosexual relationship began. The presenting analyst thought that the first analyst probably encouraged this acting out. He was an active, directive person who insisted that the patient had to break with his domineering mother in some very concrete way if he were to make progress in the analysis.

The patient married when he was in his late twenties. At first the marriage was stormy, but later evolved into a fairly good marriage. There were five children. The patient had a good emotional relationship with his wife and at times a good sexual relationship; both aspects of the relation improved in the course of analysis.

The patient held a responsible position in a large publishing concern. He worked well, especially on the administrative level, but anything that made him feel there was too great a demand on him, or conflict with an authority figure, produced acute anxiety. The anxiety attacks that initially brought him into analysis continued to be, from his subjective point of view, his real problem. Although his analysis had brought him to the realization that homosexuality was not a mature solution, he had little or no conflict about it. For example, although he realized that public knowledge of his homosexuality might be damaging, he neither worried about the possibility nor exercised much discretion about his activities. He felt that his homosexual experiences enabled him to enter into a marriage. The transference to his first analyst was intense: he still referred to him as "almost a god." His implicit sanctioning of overt homosexuality—whether it occurred in fact or in the patient's interpretation—was probably a factor in eliminating guilt.

When the patient came to his present analyst, he was struggling to curtail the homosexuality, and the struggle continued. He became able to acknowledge that his attempts to abstain were motivated not by any psychoanalytic discouragement, but by his own understanding that homosexuality, although it might have been acceptable when he was young, could no longer be regarded as a mature solution. He felt it would be more mature to improve his relations with his wife. Nevertheless, the basis of his sexual excitement was still homosexual, although in attenuated form. For a time, there would be no overt homosexual activity; then he would begin to move in that direction. First he would buy a men's magazine—one concerned with muscle building, sports, or sun culture. He would look at the photographs in which the men were naked but the penis was not exposed. The patient would become excited by looking at the photograph and then masturbate. He said that his consciousness was not focused on the penis; the strong chest was important.

After a while, photographs did not supply enough stimulation. He wanted to have some contact with a man, but believing such contact was prohibited by the analyst, he denied that he wanted it. Instead, he used a compromise technique. (The current analyst had never issued a prohibition against homosexual contact.) He would call the gym at his club, to which he used to go after his marriage, when he no longer engaged in real homosexual affairs. At this gym, he used to have a man with a beautiful physique pose for him posing would lead to mutual masturbation. Having given up visiting the gym, he substituted telephone contact with the men he knew there. He would get someone on the telephone and say, for example, "Do you still have your good body, and do you still exercise?" Sometimes he would ask about a girl he and the other man knew. This kind of conversation continued until the homosexual desire was satisfied.

The analyst reported that, since the patient had been in analysis with him, he had had only one actual homosexual affair and that, characteristically, occurred during an interruption in the analysis.

While in analysis, it suddenly occurred to the patient that he might enjoy looking at girlie magazines, and he did so. In this kind of looking, he was interested chiefly in a fetishistic symbol, the breast; but it was very important to him that the nipple and the pelvic area be covered.

During this period, his job entailed traveling. One trip took him to a foreign city, where he went to a nightclub and saw a striptease. This performance excited him so much that he masturbated in the nightclub. He also went to a striptease in the city in which he lived, and again became very excited. Afterward, he sought one girl out, had a few drinks, and talked with her. He told the analyst that this experience with the stripteaser was particularly pleasurable because he went early in the evening and few other customers were there. Apparently, the simulated excitement of the girl in the striptease was equivalent to having the girl masturbate for him; if she was excited, then he became excited. He identified with her by masturbation and did not need any direct sexual contact.

On a recent visit to another foreign city, a variation of this dynamic appeared. He went to a nightclub and saw a couple dancing. Learning that the man had been a well-known dancer when he was younger and was also a homosexual, the patient became greatly excited by watching the couple. He engaged a girl to hold his penis as he watched. She did not masturbate him to orgasm; she simply held his penis. He told the analyst proudly that this, at least, was *some* kind of relation with a girl—a great step toward heterosexuality.

One of the patient's problems was the discrepancy between his ego ideal, with its requirement of masculinity, and his homosexuality. One reason he became depressed and anxious was that he discovered that he was not courageous. He was ashamed that he was too cowardly to go into the army during the war. The ego ideal derived from his mother, who was contemptuous of his father because he was not a very good athlete. She had high ideals—a man had to be perfect in everything.

The analyst often asked, "While you have this extremely mas-culine ideal, has it never occurred to you that homosexuality is not necessarily an expression of great manliness?" The patient replied, "You don't understand. It is manly!" The analyst: "How so?" The patient: "I just look at a picture and I get an erection like a tower and I feel so powerful and potent. It makes me potent, you see, so I am manly." The patient also cited as an example a bisexual friend who had behaved with great courage during the war. The analyst agreed that to a certain extent the patient was correct: homosexu-ality and manliness are not mutually exclusive.

One member found the most interesting aspect of this case was the patient's remarkably effective incorporation defense. Merely by looking at a picture, the patient became what he saw. There were no conscious fantasies involved in this process, which occurred with extraordinary speed. The analyst considered this phenome-non—the effectiveness of the incorporative mechanism—a form of hyperfunction. The incorporative mechanism did not work indef-initely, however; after a time, the patient had to go from the picture to the real object. But as he did so, he used another sensory modal-ity, adding an auditory percept to the visual percept.

The group related this process to the ego aspect of perversion. The behavior pattern of this patient had a rhythmic character, as normal sexuality does. After a certain period, the homosexual impulse appeared spontaneously. It had a defensive quality and usually coincided with a feeling of weakness and impotence.

The analyst suggested that certain characteristics of autono-mous ego functions were responsible for the specific defenses a person used. "This kind of visual incorporative mechanism can be considered such an autonomous ego function, or ego modality, which then makes this particular defense effective for the patient. At the same time, the effectiveness of the defense may tell us some-thing about the genesis of the problem."

The analyst pointed out that the patient still fantasied that one day he would again have a genuine homosexual experience. He usually stopped before actual contact, but the progressive in-volvement—the impulse toward homosexual gratification; the act of looking at a stimulating picture; the act of making telephone contact with a man; the impulse to make physical contact with a man; and then the rejection of the impulse—this sequence still occurred periodically.

The analyst agreed that in this case the mechanism of fetishism was a defense against the perception of the female organ. He pointed out that the patient did not like to see a man dressed in woman's clothing because that aroused his castration anxiety. Fetishism was implied in that he preferred to see a man not quite naked, just as he preferred to look at photographs of women wearing fetishistic accoutrements.

Another member of the study group suggested that the esthetic contemplation of artists involved a special sensitivity to looking and to listening; that is, a sublimated use of an already eroticized ego function. The analyst thought that this observation might well apply to the patient, who felt that he failed to choose his true profession, that he should have been an industrial designer. He had a photographic memory for structural details. He was also very concerned with the decoration of his apartment, selection of art objects, choice of the color scheme, and so forth. When he inspected a manufactured object, if the design was attractive, the patient recalled it in such visual detail that the memory was eidetic.

On the other hand, the patient had what the analyst termed a mental castration complex—the need constantly to check his memory. The analyst considered this need one manifestation of heightened superego function. For example, it was extremely important that the patient read financial journals regularly. He did so, but then had to check and recheck his memory: "Do I remember? Do I remember?" He was much more concerned with whether he remembered than with what he was reading. He had the feeling that what he read and what was only in his mind was elusive. The constant fear that he could not concentrate or remember was a great problem in his business life.

The patient used perception to mold impressions according to his needs, a distortion which can be imposed upon the eidetic image, which is something between the idea and the perception. The perceptual image has the vividness and persuasiveness of a visual perception but is not fixed and objective and can be altered to meet emotional needs.

At the next meeting of the group, the analyst pointed out that little childhood or genetic material had appeared. He rejected the idea that this lack resulted from the repression by infantile amnesia. He suggested, instead, that a constitutional element played a strong role in the patient's choice of homosexuality.

Continuing his presentation, the analyst reported that although the patient was both voyeuristic and exhibitionistic, he was inhibited about using a public urinal. He claimed that he felt self-conscious because the urine didn't flow very easily, and he thought this problem might be physiological. The analyst considered this inhibition a phobic symptom arising from the patient's fear of overwhelming temptation if he were confronted by the possibility of looking at other men's penises and showing them his penis. This inhibition was constant; it was not particularly correlated with the occurrence of the perverse impulse.

The patient had another symptom, a mild depersonalization and feeling of unreality which he experienced whenever he attended the theatre. The symptom did not appear to be connected with the content of the play, nor did it occur when the patient attended a musical comedy or a ballet, because in those circumstances he derived a homosexual pleasure from looking at the men. The symptom appeared while watching dramatic theatre, and the analyst suspected that the theatre represented a primal-scene experience in which the implicit voyeurism was frightening and forbidding.

The analyst's intuition that the symptom was associated with a primal-scene fixation arose in part out of the patient's sexual acting-out. Occasionally, he hired a man and woman to perform the sexual act in his presence, and sometimes the patient himself would participate with the woman while the man watched. During an interruption in his analysis, the patient took a trip with a friend with whom he had some mild homosexual exchanges. Later, they picked up a girl and had sex *à trois*: the friend had intercourse with the girl while the patient played the voyeur; then the patient had intercourse with the girl while his friend watched.

The analyst interpreted these experiences, particularly the *à trois* episode, as a defense against both primal-scene anxiety and castration. They were all a loving family. There was no competition; the two men participated as good brothers, so to speak. Every one loved everyone. The analyst said, "The primal scene is very important. A vital part of the mechanism is that the child, under the impact of anxiety in the primal scene, has all his feelings and impulses blocked. The observing ego catches this emptiness, and that is what is partly felt, even where there is no confusion about identification. What is felt is estrangement." Resuming his report, the analyst told the group that when the patient encountered persons who could be friends, or who represented authority figures, he suddenly scrutinized himself. He thought, "How do I look? I sound wooden; my face is strange." The analyst felt that this reaction was another form of depersonalization: the patient had a voyeuristic interest in the man's penis; the interest was blocked and replaced by this depersonalized observation of himself. The analyst thought this symptom corresponded to what another group member called "regressive sexualization of the observing function of the ego and superego."

The analyst called attention to an interesting difference between the perversion and the depersonalization symptom—a question of equilibrium in defenses. The patient used certain defenses in the perversion. One of the defenses, the matter of control, was of his own making. Classically, he controlled the situation when he hired a man, told him to bring a girl, then told them what to do, and watched. When confronted with a passive experience, however, such as watching a play, he could not use such defenses; the theatre was not under his control. There, he had to look, and he seemed to turn that experience into a superego process.

The analyst suspected that this depersonalization had some relation to the displaced castration anxiety illustrated by the patient's insecurity about his memory. He was puzzled about why there had been so little genetic material from this patient. No primal-scene material had appeared directly or even indirectly except in dreams. Because his transference to this analyst was so bland, the patient did not express sexual curiosity about him.

The analyst mentioned again that the patient came into analysis not because of his perversion, but because of his anxiety. When he entered this current analysis, he had already had a previous experience in analysis, so that although the anxiety seemed somewhat diminished, it still seethed below the surface. The situations that triggered his anxiety were not manifestly sexual but were usually connected with his work—for example, when he had to face criticism by authority figures or when the demands of the job seemed overwhelming. He reacted with anxiety to a head cold because he felt that if it were a mild cold, he should go to work; if he didn't, then he was a sissy and not a man. On the other hand, if he did go to work, he was afraid that he would become seriously sick and that fear triggered anxiety. Usually, he could not decide what to do and remained in a state of anxiety and irritability.

The analysis was interrupted for a few months when the analyst left for vacation. When he returned, the patient was in a state of acute anxiety which had been triggered in part, once again, by fear of new responsibilities. This anxiety occurred in spite of the fact that the man was quite competitive. The analyst was more interested in the patient's reaction to the anxiety than in the anxiety itself. He told the study group, "It was interesting to consider what kind of castration anxiety was involved and how it worked. The patient reacted to the anxiety with extraordinary regression of the ego: he became absolutely helpless. The anxiety was not limited to fear that he would not be able to function sexually; although he often characterized it as impotency, he did not use that term in the sexual sense. He meant it in a general sense, as a feeling of utter weakness and inability to take action. He regressed to an infantile state of helplessness. This was the state in which he had decided to resume analysis. At the same time, my fetishistic power had apparently disappeared, because it seemed that the analysis had not worked if he was able to regress that far after so many years."

After the patient had settled down into the analysis again, his anxiety once more diminished. He did not develop a transference neurosis; the transference had the same quality, or served the same function, as the pictures of men. The fetishistic aspect of the transference was demonstrated by the fact that as long as he was protected by the analyst, he was protected against his severe anxiety.

The analyst wondered how the anxiety might have led to the development of the perversion. Did the perversion represent a defense against anxiety? In other words, did this man become homosexual because of the anxiety or did he develop the anxiety because he was homosexual? The analyst thought that his special ego function could not have been a causal factor in the development of the homosexuality in the same sense as the castration anxiety must have been. But he did feel that the hyperfunction—the incorporation—and timidity and sexual excitement go hand in hand. The question was whether the same fluidity of ego function shown in his perversion also had something to do with his intense anxiety, and if so, how.

The analyst emphasized that, although a homosexual episode sometimes seemed to lead to perverse acts, the patient could not resort to homosexuality when the anxiety was strongest. When there was a direct connection—for example, if a father figure on the job was critical of him and he reacted by either going to his club to find a man, or buying a magazine and masturbating—the meaning of the connection was, "I could not make my father love me; he really threatened me. My idea that I could make all men love me didn't work." The analyst thought that the patient felt very threatened, perhaps because of aggression toward other men, especially the father, and then had to reassure himself that his penis was not really in danger from other men. On the other hand, sometimes at the height of anxiety the homosexual defense was unavailable to him.

The analyst suggested the fear of the father as an element in the castration anxiety. However, the patient had not disclosed his conscious attitude toward his father, who had died when the patient was an adult. The father had been powerful and successful outside the home; the patient later discovered that his father had in many ways been a passive man.

The mother was very critical and powerful. The material the patient has brought in revealed he had two images of her, one unconscious and the other conscious. On the conscious level, he described his mother as a strong person, "like a man"; a phallic mother, critical of and slightly satirical about the father's clumsiness in making repairs about the house. But in the patient's dreams the analyst found the image of the castrated mother. The patient was not aware of the meaning of a recurrent dream about rescue on the water. In his recurrent dream, he rescued the mother from some kind of boat, water, or storm.

The patient relied on his mother inordinately. For example, "My mother always told me everything I should do. I relied on her even to tell me how much pepper and salt I should put on my steak." However, he identified with the castrated mother in the anxiety state. In other words, in this patient, incorporation related to both the positive and negative fantasies which underlay the perversion; when the patient said that he was impotent, he meant it anatomically—that he did not have a penis. The image did not become conscious, but the analyst believed that a strong image of the castrated mother existed in his unconscious.

At the next meeting of the group, the analyst returned to the patient's initial experience in homosexuality. Recently the analyst had asked: "Do you think you would have become homosexual if you had not gone into analysis?" To his surprise, the patient answered, "No." Yet he does not blame his homosexuality on the analyst; he blesses him for it. When the analyst asked how the analysis could have facilitated the homosexuality, the patient replied, "The analyst didn't encourage me directly, but he also didn't discourage me." The analyst felt that the dynamics were more complex than the patient's explanation indicated.

The patient's transference to his first analyst was the most intense he had experienced. This first analyst emphasized the bad mother theory. He told the patient that he had to spit in his mother's face. "You will have to tell your mother how she ruined you and that will set you free." The analyst felt that this was an example of the introjection of the superego. Until the patient first entered analysis, his superego figure was his mother. She made all the demands. The analyst then constituted a new superego figure who helped him rebel against the superego of the mother. The only way he could do so was to introject a new superego—the analyst—to do battle against the mother.

In connection with his mother, the patient reported an incident that had occurred recently. His mother was now very old. The patient was talking about her to some of his friends. One friend remarked, "Don't you remember, your mother used to laugh a lot?" The patient said, "I don't remember, but I don't think she does that any more." The analyst then asked him when his mother's laughter had disappeared. The patient answered, "Come to think about it, after I attacked her, at the bidding of my analyst."

The analyst felt that this story confirmed his hypothesis: the patient felt unable to live up to his mother's demands that he be courageous and masculine. But he was able to rebel against her only by introjecting as superego the analyst, who was an even more dominating personality than his mother.

The analyst referred to an invisible connection between the

first analyst, the mother, and the first homosexual partner. He thought that the homosexual affair was a grandiose acting-out because even the choice of a homosexual partner was determined by features relating to both the analyst and the mother. There was a common denominator, which the analyst did not define for reasons of discretion, that made the relationship highly probable.

Another curious parallel lay in the patient's reason for leaving the first analyst. The patient was utterly devoted to him, but when the analyst left for a long summer vacation, the patient felt he was in serious trouble and was unable to forgive the abandonment. As in his first homosexual affair, he could not tolerate not being the analyst's most important concern.

The analyst continued: "The difference between harboring perverse fantasies and indulging in perversion was the difference between a superego that would tolerate the perversion and one that would not. This patient's fantasy life was remarkably inhibited, a fact which I found puzzling. I wondered whether there was an inverse relation between the prevalence of perverse fantasies and overt perverse behavior expressed first in fantasy. Did the fantasy become translatable at one point into actual behavior? I wanted to suggest that perhaps an additional factor should have been taken into account: an intensification of the drive in the transference relationship may have triggered homosexual activity at that particular point in the patient's life."

In answer to a question about the patient's reaction to the interpretations the analyst had made, the analyst reported that there had been no response. The patient was so blocked that even when the analyst tried to show him how the complex had to be related to his feelings about his mother, the patient was unable to recognize what the analyst was saying.

The analyst felt that the first transference had encouraged the patient's homosexuality and he believed the patient was sincere in thinking he would not have become homosexual if he had not gone into analysis. Nevertheless, the analyst felt that, in view of the intensity, spontaneity, and instinctual nature of the homosexual drive, the patient would have become homosexual at some point in his life without any external influence. One member of the group suggested that the first analyst felt that this man was inhibited in action and therefore encouraged him to act out something, perhaps feeling that acting-out was preferable to inhibition. The analyst agreed that this might have been the case, particularly in view of the patient's belief that, without the first homosexual experience, he would not have been able to marry.

The analyst continued his discussion of the transference in the perversion. He had told the group that when the analysis had been interrupted, the patient had immediately resumed homosexual practices. At a later date, when the analyst was away, the patient again arranged a trip related to his business affairs. Again, he was very tempted by homosexual impulses. He went to a public swimming pool and saw two boys to whom he was intensely attracted. Although he talked to them, he was too inhibited to act, and felt tremendous conflict. He was not sure whether the boys were homosexual, but he would have found out if his inhibition had not been so strong and the conflict so intense. He returned to his hotel, and was tempted to ask the bellboy to send him a girl. He did not want to have intercourse with her, but he wanted her to pose or perform a striptease. He curbed that impulse too, but he did masturbate. When he returned home, he had an unusually satisfying sexual experience with his wife. The entire experience left him both stimulated and satisfied because he had found that he could exercise a certain amount of control, and he enjoyed a feeling of mastery and heightened self-esteem. A short time before the analyst's return, however, the patient became jittery and tense, evidently feeling anxiety and guilt. He told the analyst about the episode.

The analyst interpreted both the episode and the patient's reaction as transference phenomena. First, homosexual acting-out occurred when the analysis was interrupted, an indication that the transference represented identification with a powerful phallic figure by whom the patient felt protected. The guilt resulting from contemplating homosexual activity was particularly interesting in that the patient had always maintained that he felt no guilt about his homosexuality. The guilt in this instance was a transference phenomenon in that the analyst was working with him on overcoming the problem of homosexuality. The analyst commented that it was remarkable that the patient, even while he displayed serious resistance, nevertheless improved. He cited as proof the fact that the patient was in a state of near-psychosis when he returned after the interruption of the analysis. In contrast, during the current year while under continuing treatment, the patient had been successful at work, more or less free of anxiety, and fairly satisfied in his relationship with his wife. The analyst considered this result a transference cure, without sufficient insight. He accepted the patient's claim that he did not feel guilt about his homosexuality, but he believed that it was a subjective statement. The guilt was expressed in the patient's constant expectation that he would be criticized on his job and that he would fail to live up to expectations; the analyst also felt that the guilt was connected more closely with masturbation than with the homosexuality. This interpretation, too, the patient rejected: "I didn't feel guilty; I just thought that it was not healthy or could do me some harm." The analyst interpreted this statement as an expression of castration anxiety.

At this point, one member of the group suggested that the patient was an obedient man who denied awareness of any protest by his superego. He cited the patient's experience in school, when he responded to his father's letter by improving his grades. In the same fashion, the patient may have been responding to his increased desire for the absent analyst by first feeling an impulse toward homosexual behavior and then partially satisfying himself by masturbating. He then might have become apprehensive, not because he felt guilt with respect to the analyst's superego, but simply because he was afraid of his criticism.

The analyst felt that this theory was not entirely accurate. Something had really changed in the patient; he had a different attitude toward homosexuality. The change was not just obedience, but insight of a fetishistic quality. To the patient, acquiring insight meant borrowing power from the man in an illusory way; in this sense, he did develop some insight. He now rejected homosexuality not simply in moral terms, but because it was an infantile and immature act, and he wished and needed to become more mature.

The analyst also pointed out that the patient now displayed castration anxiety in addition to guilt. This anxiety was revealed in the sequence of events during the recent interruption of analysis: the homosexual temptation, the satisfying sexual experience with his wife, and the subsequent build-up of anxiety before the analyst's return. The analyst suggested that the perversion first quieted the castration anxiety and then stimulated it, but he was uncertain about the pathway of the stimulation. He hypothesized that strong, passive feelings after the homosexual experience made the patient afraid of losing his penis. He did not feel that the castration anxiety could be explained simply as fear of punishment by the analyst or the father.

In reply to a question about the nature of the transference just before the separation, the analyst said that he and the patient were in a loving phase because he represented the powerful, manly figure. Although the patient did not acknowledge the analyst's personal influence, he said the analysis helped him. Whatever fantasy wishes he had toward the analyst were repressed—one of the problems in analyzing him.

The analyst felt that the upsurge of conflict and homosexual desire following separation from the analyst was partly a matter of "when the cat's away the mice will play." These episodes occurred not only when the analyst was away, but also when the patient's wife was away. At such times, he was usually tempted to buy some magazines and make some telephone calls.

The analyst suggested that another pathway for the development of castration anxiety was the fear of castration by the father. The anxiety could be based on the fantasy of taking away the father's penis. If the perversion had this function, then obviously the patient would be afraid that retaliation would follow after he acted out. The analyst also discerned another element which emerged less clearly: that some feminine identification—a desire to be female, to be overwhelmed—must have been stirred up. This element related to the body image complex, but if it did in fact exist, it remained repressed in the patient's mind.

Another member of the group offered the opinion that, in view of the success of the analysis, the magic of the perversion was being spoiled for the patient; he could no longer maintain the notion that he could become a superman by incorporating pictures of muscle men. If so, the anxiety-binding feature of the perversion may have been failing, and that may have been part of the reason the patient became anxious.

The analyst concurred in this formulation but called it successful analysis of the defense. Since the patient married and had children he has experienced more open anxiety. He was particularly affectionate toward his sons, and he asked the analyst whether his open affection would predispose them to homosexuality. For this reason, the analyst felt that maturation too had played a role in undermining the anxiety-binding function of the perversion.

The analyst agreed with another member of the group that separation anxiety also occurred when the analyst was away. He referred to the fact that separation anxiety was a critical factor in the first analysis. The patient required an object and was unable to create one out of his own resources. He needed to be stimulated to mental activity through some outside force. This need for outside stimulation demonstrated great dependence upon the object, as did the transference relationship. Possibly, this need for concrete contact with the object was an element in the patient's homosexual acting-out when the analyst was away.

On the other hand, the analyst pointed out, he had no material indicating an early experience of object loss. The patient was not separated from his mother or father when he was a child, and he always had a nurse taking care of him. Furthermore, he was well able to tolerate being sent to boarding school at a comparatively early age.

At this point another member of the group pointed out that, in discussing object relations, it was necessary to define terms. For example, an infant has a very intense object relation, but it is not similar to the object relation in an adult. One may be looking at an object relationship that isn't entirely tenuous, but has a pathologic quality, a preoccupation with a certain kind of instinctual aim. The instinctual quality may be preeminently egocentric or highly narcissistic, but in that sense it is still a kind of object relation.

He went on to suggest that there are two extreme patterns of perversion, most actual cases lying on a continuum between the two. First, there are individuals who develop a perversion predominantly on the basis of fixation, associated with a certain plasticity, occurring at a crucial time in their development. Under specific and favorable circumstances, there may be relatively little depression or guilt. These individuals would not be apt to consult an analyst unless they had difficulty with the law; their problems are conflicts with society, not intrapsychic conflicts. At the other extreme, there is the perversion that is very close to a neurotic symptom, in which the symptomatic expressions—anxiety, depression, and guilt—are displaced from the genital, or sexual zone into a substitute activity, such as a work inhibition. The suggestion implicit in this observation was that the case under consideration fell closer to the latter end of the continuum described.

In his final discussion of the patient, the analyst focused on the patient's marriage. He reminded the group that the patient married at about the age of twenty-eight years. His wife was pretty, at least during the early years of the marriage. Although the marriage was stormy at first, it improved during the years of analysis. The analyst suggested that this improvement may have occurred because the sexual disturbances were more fully analyzed than in the previous analysis, and the patient in some way learned to channel some of his earlier fantasies into his heterosexual life.

The patient rarely experienced spontaneous desire for his wife, but when he did have intercourse, he had no potency difficulty. He and his wife both derived pleasure from the intercourse. If he had no spontaneous erection, his wife engaged in sex play until an erection was achieved. There was, however, always some undercurrent of fear, although not a fear of how he would perform; nor was the fear strong enough to cause any potency difficulty. He did ask his wife to introduce a dowel into his anus during intercourse. The analyst interpreted this wish as a desire to play both roles, and apparently the interpretation frightened the patient because he abandoned the activity.

When he interrupted his analysis, the heterosexual activities diminished greatly in both intensity and frequency. During the previous summer, his marriage had become especially stormy. The analyst believed that, when the patient was alone with his wife, he missed the compensation of his work and his contact with men, and this loss was a factor in provoking quarrels. The patient's major complaint against his wife, which was a realistic one, was that she was ineffectual.

His wife's passivity infuriated the patient. He said that her ineffectuality rendered him impotent. The analyst felt that his impotence resulted from his inability to force her to do what he wanted. He also suspected that the patient was disturbed by the contrast between his efficient, well-organized mother and his inefficient wife. Moreover, since his wife was so inefficient, she did not serve as a model with whom he could identify so as to compensate for his own weakness. He tended, therefore, to identify with the castrated wife who refused to become more efficient.

Typically, he used fantasies to stimulate his potency. In one, he imagined wrestling with one of his muscle men and pinning him to the floor. The fantasy gave the patient such a feeling of power that he was able to enjoy intercourse with his wife. On another occasion, while staying in the country, he remained unshaven and nursed a fantasy of being like a character in a D. H. Lawrence book. Identifying with a strong, virile man again facilitated pleasurable intercourse.

When he looked at girlie magazines, he was most interested in pictures of women who had large, well-developed breasts. The relation to the breast was mostly visual: on occasions when women actually posed for him, he rarely even touched the breast. Looking was the important element.

Although the patient remained very much attached to his wife and to his children, sexual desire diminished and intercourse became less frequent. Usually, when he repressed homosexuality and resisted his perverse interests, desire for his wife disappeared too.

The analyst proposed that there were two factors in this case which were of general importance for the problem of homosexuality and perversion. One was the element of visual perception and imagery; the other was the element of the visual incorporative mechanism for male homosexuality, which the analyst thought was not a genetic factor in the psychologic sense, but a defensive factor. He considered such a defense an important element in reinforcing the fixation, which was difficult to dissolve because it gave this patient a powerful, albeit momentary, reassurance against castration anxiety and a reassuring feeling of potency and virility that allowed discharge of sexual excitement. The analyst felt that in this case at least, the mechanism became automatic once it was established.

Another member of the group commented particularly on visual imagery, emphasizing the part it played in establishing the image of the self. In the case of this individual, his childhood self-image was of someone small, scrawny, and ineffective with a small boy's penis and an unmasculine body. He felt confronted by an enormous and challenging woman who required him to be a superman. This member suggested that the body-image had a delusional value or affect in that it was a fixed idea, unchanged by the development and progression of the patient's own masculinity through the years, even though he had become quite a different person from that little boy.

The presenting analyst agreed with this hypothesis and added, "Not only was his body-image unchanging, but his self-image as well, because he did not appreciate the fact that he held a responsible position and was a successful businessman." He added one further note to the discussion of the visual image. The patient could facilitate an erection by looking at his mirror image, particularly if he put on a bikini. But apparently the mirror image could not be integrated; the internal self-image and the body-image remained unchanged in their childhood form.

CASE III

E.F., a fourteen-year-old boy, has been in analysis for six years. He attends a private school, and—before he began treatment—psychologically sensitive members of the school staff had attempted for years to persuade the boy's parents that he needed help. The school's perception of the boy was that he was unhappy, emotionally uninvolved, withdrawn, clumsy, shy, frightened, and overcompliant. Furthermore, when he became involved in a discussion, he would pursue a subject interminably, insistently, and in a style that obscured the original point. But his parents did not actually bring him in for treatment until he himself requested it.

He had been tested at various ages and recalled hating both the psychologists he had seen at those times. Because E. had been followed psychologically from infancy by a psychoanalytically oriented pediatrician, and from the onset of his enrollment in an observationally oriented nursery school, the analyst had much early data and many direct observations about his behavior as well as test results and reports of conferences with his parents.

E. is the elder of two children; his sister is three and a half years younger than he. At the time he entered treatment, his father was about forty-one and his mother about thirty-seven years old. His father, an only child, had been born in Sweden, was educated both abroad and in the United States, and is an American citizen. He had worked in international banking, and after that had joined a firm that specialized in economic consultation with import-export firms. The mother, a college graduate, had been a home economist and a member of a domestic science research team.

When E. entered treatment, all his grandparents were alive. His paternal grandparents were Swedish; his maternal grandparents were born in the United States. The paternal grandmother and the maternal grandfather died when the boy was about twelve years old.

During the first year and a half of the child's life, the family lived in an apartment in a house owned by his uncle. Since then, his family has occupied only one apartment, although they spent summers at various summer places. E. has been cared for primarily by his parents, but also by one nurse and one maid, and occasionally by one or more of his grandparents.

The boy is right-handed; he sat at seven months, walked at thirteen months; talked in sentences at seventeen months, and had a one-hundred-ten word vocabulary by the time he was twenty months old. He was an active infant who had been breast fed for three or four months and then received a bottle until his sister was born. After her birth, he was given a bottle only at bedtime. He was on demand-feeding schedule as an infant and his weaning was simple. However, he liked to be helped with eating, at least until the time he was brought into treatment.

E. had had a painful teething period and had cried a great deal at night. He wanted to be held, but suddenly, between the ages of two and two and a half years old, he began to withdraw periodically and progressively from physical contact. His toilet training was allegedly easy and rather late.

Early in his life he developed a fear of noises, such as those made by boats, engines, and subways. He was also afraid of large groups of people. He had been taken to a motion picture theatre at an early age and afterward occasionally showed fear of motion picture screens. He was also afraid of playground and athletic equipment.

The analyst reported that E. had had fears of motion all his life: fears of having his body move unexpectedly; of being dropped; of having rugs pulled out from under him; of slipping on floors; of being attacked by people or animals. The fear seemed to center on anxiety about being pushed off balance.

In the child's early play, he was preoccupied with mechanical things such as phonograph records, spinning wheels, electrical appliances, and particularly electric cords. He also had two stuffed animals to which he had some attachment.

The analyst was told that from the time E. began to speak, he was preoccupied with verbalisms, phrases, styles of speech, and intellectual concepts. He engaged in observation rather than action, and was preoccupied with safety and security rather than risk-taking and experimentation.

His parents always handled him by what they call "explanation, substitution, and guidance." They seldom ordered him directly, commanded him directly, punished him directly, or showed direct affective expression of disapproval; and they discouraged affective reaction from the child himself. The parents' method of child-rearing was determined both by their ideological convictions and by their temperaments. The analyst discovered that the parents were experts at circumlocution: neither could give a direct answer to any question.

The families of both parents were gifted people. The paternal grandfather was an émigré who returned to Europe after World War I, stayed there for a while, and then came back to the United States and rejoined his family. Members of the family have enjoyed eminence and success in the literary, the scholarly, and the political world.

The analyst felt that there were a number of prognostic elements in the case that are often encountered in children likely to become either psychotic or autistic. For example, as a little boy E. tended to rock himself to sleep. But he never developed the classical picture: he did not have the total absence of eye contact, and was not globally withdrawn. However, he developed styles of social retreat very early, and he still used them.

E. had difficulty doing anything technological. Although he was interested in mechanical objects, his interest was in watching them and seeing how they worked. He made both auditory and visual observations. The analyst thought his interest extended also to vibratory and kinesthetic perceptivity. E. was preoccupied with the vibrations he felt in buildings; he knew when an elevator was moving; he knew when a train was moving underneath the streets.

One of the reasons the boy had been brought into treatment was that he had become progressively more preoccupied with an imaginary universe which was peopled, had its own currency, its own police force, its own rules, its own laws, and its own newspaper, which he published. He was spending more time developing this fantasy world than he gave to anything else. He was withdrawing from his friends and from activities with his family, and locking himself in his room to create this world. He did, however, get up every morning and go to school.

A psychoanalyst had examined him twice, and then referred him to the current analyst. She had described him as being so terror stricken at their first meeting that he had fled from her office after a few minutes contact and could not be persuaded to return, even with his mother. On the second contact with the referring psychoanalyst, he was trembling with fright and overpowering anxiety. The reporting analyst, however, found him much less bizarre on the surface than the description of the referring psychoanalyst indicated.

The boy had been prodigiously literary from the age of six years on. He had dictated a book to an adult about an imaginary universe in which people were transmuted. The story employed themes from *Gulliver's Travels, Superman, Alice in Wonderland;* it also utilized aerial transportation independent of vehicles, and magical reversals of identity from fascist to communist. There were two specific precipitating causes, from the parents' point of view, for bringing the boy into treatment. The mother was concerned by his tantrums, which he would throw in public places. The father had a veiled, but later overt, suspicion that the boy was becoming homosexual. When the father finally discussed this concern with the analyst, he alluded to it coyly, as if attempting to make the analyst say the word or guess what the father had in mind before he finally declared what his fear actually was. The father claimed that he was afraid of homosexuality in his son because the boy was awkward in movements and had a rather baby-like face, soft musculature, and large buttocks. The father had a similar build. In discussing this with the analyst, the father elaborately explained that the boy was exactly like himself and then said, "Guess what's the matter with him?" He seemed to be challenging the analyst to make some remark about his own sexuality.

The imaginary world E. created was a historical scheme that involved the history of the United States, world history, and international and interplanetary history. He had assigned a special code word to everything, such as currency units; he had designed flags, money, and imaginary people; he kept records of election voting totals; he had made maps of his imaginary countries and continually changed the maps, as boundaries changed in the course of political events. The parents had finally found the situation intolerable.

When E. was five years old, he was examined by a psychologist, and the examination disclosed an I.Q. of 154. At that time, he was greatly preoccupied with power. The psychologist saw him as an anxious, depressed child, unable to express his feelings, compulsively evasive, and using all his energy in this compulsion. He saw the world as threatening; he exhibited many fears, sexual confusion, sexual preoccupation, and confusion of sexual identity; he displayed a gloomy quality in all his drawings and his interpretations of the drawings of others. The psychologist found a rather metaphysical fairytale quality to his fantasies. The psychologist felt that he was a seriously disturbed child and needed help, but at that time was unable to convince the parents.

For years the parents had a deep reluctance to believe that their son required treatment, although it had been suggested when he was three or four years old, and urged from the time he was four until he was eight. The parents rationalized: the mother said that she herself had been slow in learning to talk; the father said that he, too, had been slow in athletics. Actually, the boy was not slow in athletics; while he was seemingly and intermittently clumsy, he was terribly competitive. On the other hand, if he was allowed to win, or even if he really won accidently, he felt insulted, because he always assumed, in a rather paranoid, masochistic fashion, that he couldn't possibly win and that hence the competitor was belittling him and being condescending.

The parents presented separate and quite different observations of the child over the years. The father felt that he never really connected with the child, especially at times of crisis. He claimed that the boy was always in command of the situation. Yet, though the father presented himself as being unable to manage the boy, his manner was one of always being in command of both the boy and of the wife. The mother, on the other hand, looked very helpless, yet talked as if she had everything under control and all the boy needed was to be handled her way. Essentially, they described the same thing, but they used different terminology.

The parents also suspected that E. was teasing his sister, but they could not confirm their suspicion. It was months before the analyst could get them to tell him what was going on between E. and his sister, which turned out to be a complicated, ritualistic kind of sex play.

The boy felt compelled to read the newspaper every day before school. He felt that the world would fall apart if he weren't on top of the news. The analyst sensed that the parents had a deadly fear of disagreeing directly with this child; that they always handled him tangentially. For example, at every meal, particularly one at which there were dinner guests, he would manage to knock over a pitcher, spill a plate, or overturn someone's glass—always in a semi-innocent and defensive manner that communicated that he must not, even by implication, be accused of being in error. Over the years, the parents attributed this provocative behavior to lack of fine motor coordination; they never suggested that he had any responsibility for these actions.

The parents reported that E. had had difficulty in swallowing when he was three years old; that he reacted with panic to any change in plans or to any delay. In the course of describing the situation with their son to the analyst, the parents talked vaguely of deaths and sickness in the extended family and became involved in pointless discussions about dates and identities.

At the time the boy entered treatment, his paternal grandfather was living with the family about half the time. The parents were primarily concerned that treatment might "hurt the boy's morale"— a fear the analyst interpreted as meaning that it might hurt his status in class.

Except in one or two brief panic scenes, the analyst had never seen the boy quite as disturbed as the referring psychoanalyst had described him. The analyst suggested that the reason might have been a difference in the way the boy presented himself to a man and to a woman. The boy had told the woman psychoanalyst that there were lots of schizoid people in the family and had gone on to describe them almost clinically, in an obsessional way.

At this point in the presentation the analyst displayed several drawings done by E. when he was ten years old. The drawings were very primitive; in one, a person had six fingers on one hand and about eight on the other. The analyst was more interested in the boy's perception of his drawings than in his drawing skill. He told the study group that most kids would say, "I don't draw very well," but E. made no such statement.

In his first interview with the analyst, the boy was restless. He had a gait that might be called waddling, and gave the impression that he might bump against the wall. He was engaged in some kind of energy discharge and spent a great deal of time twisting his clothing, tying and untying his shoestrings, sometimes partially unlacing his shoes and then relacing them. His speech was scattered, but always relevant. He spoke about baseball, about friends at school, about the place he had spent the summer. Finally, after getting acquainted and talking about what kinds of things E. liked to do, the analyst said, "How come you are here?" The boy said, "I get mad pretty easy. If I don't do as well—if I do or don't do as well as I can do, or I used to . . ." The analyst asked, "Well, for example?" The boy replied, "I can't recall examples. There was one a long time ago." Then he said, 'I cry and argue and I try to make a point that the other person is wrong." The analyst thought the boy touched on one of his problems in this statement—he spent a great deal of time trying to prove the analyst wrong.

The boy then jumped to talking about the time of year and what he was looking forward to. It was close to Halloween and he said he wore a mummy costume last Halloween. He said he was studying the United Nations. The analyst asked why he had jumped from Halloween to the United Nations and the boy replied, "U.N.I.C.E.F. has the trick-or-treat boxes." He then said that he was never hurt, he never won or lost, and never teased, except in fun. He was never teased, and last year he liked the man teacher better than the woman teacher. This year he liked the woman teacher.

The analyst asked him what he did for fun. The boy replied, "Outside, I play ball; inside, I play board games; and by myself, I read." He revealed nothing to the analyst about his newspaper and his private world for many months, although the analyst gave him many opportunities and occasionally almost hinted at it. Asked what he liked to read, the boy replied, "Well, it isn't too easy for me, I like exciting books and funny books, like Eleanor Roosevelt's book on her life." The analyst considered this an odd statement from a ten-year-old.

He mentioned friends who attended the same school. The analyst noted that he had a superior vocabulary. The boy told the analyst that he wanted to be an engineer; he liked designing things and houses. He drew a house; the drawing was as primitive as those of the man and woman the analyst had shown the group.

When he drew the man and woman, the analyst asked, "Well, how are they different?" The boy replied, "Men are more manly." When asked if he would like to see the analyst again, he said he would. He almost assumed he was going to and began demanding all the appointments, but the analyst ended the session by saying that they would get acquainted in order to see what ought to be done and whether the analyst could be of help to him.

In the second session, the boy began talking about a weekend in the mountains, about sailing on a lake, and about being with his relatives. He told the analyst that his grandfather had died the previous June. In reality, the grandfather had died three years earlier, but the boy was confused about the dates of his grandparents' deaths and the confusion persisted. The analyst then asked the boy to tell him more about himself. He replied, "My father's in economic consultation; I want to be an engineer. I know one father who has friends who are designers. Father's father lives with us." Then, "I don't want to talk anymore. Let's play checkers." They spent the rest of the session playing two slow games of checkers. The boy was compulsive, constantly changing his moods, and preoccupied with rules and strategy, but, as the analyst described it, one could hear the wheels clanking as he played. He wasn't a smooth player and he did not seem to have much fun. His motor clumsiness was very prominent in the way he handled the checkers. He showed an intention tremor that made it difficult for him actually to grasp the checker; yet he could tie and untie his shoe laces very skillfully.

In the next interview the patient came in and announced almost proudly that he had had a fight the previous Sunday, but he couldn't remember what it was about. The analyst asked with whom he had fought, and the boy replied, "I can remember—it was with Mother and Father. Father said, "Let's go,' and asked me to zip up my zipper." The analyst asked him what happened then. He replied, "I was mostly mad inside." The analyst: "What made you mad?" "Well, it wasn't necessary to tell me to zip up my zipper." The analyst considered this reaction injured innocence; the boy was outraged at being given excessive instructions. The boy then went on to talk about nightmares. He said that he had had no dreams in a long time. Then he reported a dream he had had a long time ago. A couple of days before the dream he had been on a subway with a friend and had seen a drunken person. In the dream, the drunken person had come into the house and killed the boy's sister. The boy didn't know how. After telling the dream, he turned to the analyst and said, "And so." The analyst waited. Then the boy said, "Then we had to get out of the house, outside the house; it was full of steps in a wide street. Everyone was saying something about the Civil War." The analyst interpreted this as another instance when his preoccupation with nations and wars and history, expressed his hostility toward his love objects.

From the third interview on, E. showed considerable interest in dreams and wanted to discuss his own theory about dreams with the analyst at some length, which the analyst permitted him to do. In this session E. continued, "I also had a dream when I knew I was dreaming. It was a sort of river and kept flowing down, and all of a sudden everything was on a light pole. I knew I was dreaming. It was early morning and I was half asleep and there were people with letters and the river kept on flowing and I wasn't happy or sad." The analyst asked if he could tell him more about it. The boy replied, "It was a long time ago." He said, "Sometimes at night, especially in the country, if I wake up in the middle of the night, sometimes I think that our house has been taken over by robbers, especially during windstorms." He gave, as an example, a recent hurricane. The boy drew a clumsy layout of his bed and bedroom which bore no resemblance to subsequent, more accurate drawings.

What struck the analyst about this session was that, while E. was talking about a hurricane, he recalled an occasion, when he was two or three years old, when he and other children went out on the beach and picked up stinking fish that had washed up. As he talked about this, he began to handle his genitals. It was the first time the analyst had seen this kind of behavior. He was sitting sprawled in a chair; the analyst described his posture as awkward and gratuitously clumsy, not the typical adolescent slouch. The analyst said, "He made himself look, act, and seem almost doltish or physically stupid. It was almost an imitation of a neurological disorder."

In the same interview the analyst asked him the conventional question: 'If you had three wishes, what would you wish?" E. replied, "One, for a lot more wishes." To a query about the second wish: "Then I have to think." To the query about the third wish: "Well, if there are only three, well, I don't know." In the analyst's experience, this was an unusual reaction to the question, but typical of children who are protecting their secret thoughts and who have trouble letting anyone know what they want. The whole dimension of wanting is eliminated.

During this session, the lights in the analyst's apartment went out. The analyst went down to see whether he could replace the fuse. He had left the boy with a flashlight. When the analyst returned, he found that the boy had been drawing persons by the light of the flashlight. The analyst asked him about boys and girls. He replied, "A boy could be more brave; also probably he will like athletics more and the girl will like dolls and stuff more; she can do more female stuff and the man usually works and the woman sometimes works and she usually does house stuff and she can have babies and she acts more interested in the way things look, like clothes and the way people dress and act."

He claimed to have no hobbies. The analyst thought the patient considered his question about hobbies as a form of trial. The analyst then said, "Do you ever make models?" The patient replied, "Sometimes." This was the closest the analyst came to asking him outright about his fantasy world.

In a subsequent hour, the boy asked the analyst if he would take dictation. But when he started dictating, each statement qualified the previous one.

At the close of this presentation, the analyst summarized the perverse manifestations he eventually discovered in the boy's behavior. At one point, he had created a codpiece for himself; at other times he had created breasts, and had been preoccupied in costuming his sister. A final symptom was the boy's insistence on taking literal precautions against fantasy and dream characters and against possible intrusions into the apartment during the night. These precautions included arrangements of doorknobs and bathrooms and, later on, a whole system for identifying homosexual versus heterosexual impulses in both the male and the female.

At the next meeting of the study group, one member suggested that E.'s creation of a magic world was characteristic of an earlier stage. He wondered how much reality it had for the boy—whether it was not fantasy, but an expression of omnipotence. The analyst pointed out that the boy had started creating magic worlds when he was three or four years old, when he dictated stories to his mother.

Another member of the study group suggested that this creation of a private world served the purpose of anxiety control; that he needed to fabricate an artificial world in which he was the sole determiner of events. He wondered whether this pervasive ego position vis-à-vis his drive would have an effect upon his body representation, making fluid his realistic perception of his body, so that the boy fluctuated between the extremes of male and female.

The study group then asked the analyst whether he had any material about sex in this magical world.

The analyst replied that the only information about sex had come out in the boy's dreams. In one, for example, the boy and his family were in a taxi driving on a strange road. The other members of his family were undifferentiated in this dream. (This was one of the patient's problems: he sometimes called his mother "Father" and his father, "Mother," and he confused himself with his sister.) In the dream, a man was standing by the road holding a baby. He hailed the taxi and handed the baby over to the people in it. In E.'s association to the dream, he revealed the fantasy that babies were given away, that they were available from either men or women, and that they could be given to children. The members of the study group speculated that, for this boy, reality was still something that could be manufactured. In that sense, there was nothing really fixed in his sexuality: he was neither a boy nor a girl, neither a man nor a woman.

The analyst concurred and related a fantasy the boy had about a teacher who changed from a male to a female. In the fantasy, the female teacher was exercising some kind of subversive influence on him that would turn him into a female—some kind of thought control or transmission or contagious femininity. She wanted him to become a girl and would make him into a girl, but she was unaware of this. He, however, was aware of it and had to fight to avoid catching her femininity.

Another member of the study group suggested that the patient's striking clumsiness corresponded to a drive inhibition, to inhibition of more aggressive behavior.

The analyst agreed, except that the inhibition did not apply in one situation: when E. and his sister were in the elevator in their apartment building. Then and then only, was he able to attack— verbally, gesturally, and with physical violence. He would contrive to be in the same elevator with his sister so that he could shock, frighten, or beat her and yet arrive at his door looking quite digni- fied and stupid and clumsy. In the meantime he would have reduced her to complete submission or forced her to regain her composure. Apparently she obeyed his orders to regain her composure, because for a long time her parents believed she had been only pretending that her brother made these attacks on her. In retrospect, the analyst thought the boy actually molested his sister sexually, although he could not verify his suspicion. The parents could not determine whether this was true; their son would not admit it. E. started to have dreams about stabbing and murdering his sister.

Replying to the question of whether the boy's private world was rigid and formalized, the analyst observed that, while it was to some degree, it also had imaginative and highly detailed creative aspects. The boy was able to integrate elements from the real world, from the family history, from political ideology, and from mysti- cism; and he did not do so in an entirely bizarre or arbitrary manner. He did world history for the past two hundred years. The analyst said that the magical world was not stereotyped, but neither was it completely creative; it was a dwarfed and distorted or disguised originality.

It was almost impossible to elicit guilt in E. If he was badly thought of by others, or imagined that he would be, or if he was exposed, he would feel ashamed; not, however, in terms of having done something wrong or of deserving punishment. Exposure would make him feel so ashamed and humiliated that he would either have to kill someone or feel that he himself had to be killed. This would not be punishment; it would be the elimination of a shame too humiliating to live with.

The analyst felt that the boy enjoyed his fantasy world but recognized that it was so off-beat that he was ashamed to reveal it, even to the analyst, although he suggested it in riddles, symbols, colors, and obscure codes.

E. used omnipotent fantasies as compensation for his feeling of impotence in the physical world and at the same time used the impotence to control his aggressiveness. The tantrums that had so disturbed his mother practically ceased, and the only aggression he continued to show was his tormenting of his sister.

The analyst then described the first real panic the boy had admitted to him. It was a muted, controlled panic which arose while the boy was watching a school play in which his sister appeared on stage wearing a leotard and a T-shirt decorated with a picture of a monster. The incident occurred when the boy was about eleven or twelve years old. His sister was one of many performers. The patient was sitting next to a boy and became so uncomfortable that he had to get up and go to the toilet to urinate. It took him almost two and a half hours to tell the analyst about this incident, and the analyst had to reconstruct many details with supplementary information from the parents. He learned, for example, the boy himself had been in the school performance. He seemed to have been most upset about his sister's behavior during rehearsals. She had been doing a lot of exhibitionistic dancing, and he finally admitted that what upset him so was that other boys could see her exposed in this manner. They might think that he had fantasies about her, and he had to get out of the auditorium before the fantasies became evident. The analyst suggested that he was really saying he was afraid he would have an erection and the boys would see it. The boy did not deny this interpretation.

The analyst later learned that E. had participated much more directly in this entire situation. He had rewritten the lines assigned to his sister, rewritten his own lines, and it was he who had induced her to wear the T-shirt with the monster on it rather than the costume she was supposed to wear. His panic then arose because he was afraid that he would be exposed as having created this fantasy—his reaction was shame, not guilt. In a curious reversal, he thought that if the boys learned that he was excited by the scene, they would think that he was a girl.

After he became embarrassed about the possibility of having an erection, he made a codpiece for himself. He started tying knots in his shirt so that it would look as if his penis were bigger and knots in his undershirt to simulate breasts. Then he made prosthetic devices to simulate breasts and penises, using foam rubber, plastic, and cellophane. Finally these devices became so exaggerated that the father admitted they were obscene.

The analyst saw the genesis of this perverse behavior in the parents' implied enjoyment of the sister's capacity to excite the boy and the male manifestations of arousal in their son, who they feared was homosexual. In a sense, they provided him with a sexual object in the hope that it would help him to polarize himself sexually. (Actually, it made him ambivalent, confused, and frightened.) Part of his need to polarize himself stemmed from the fact that the father was more maternal than the mother; the mother felt that she was inadequately feminine. Consequently, both worried about the sexual polarization of their children. Although they vaguely recognized that this was not beneficial to either the daughter or the son, they found it hard to disentangle themselves from the boy's behavior, because in analysis he would expose their sexual problems. They reported the transvestite—or hermaphrodite—behavior six months after it had started.

At about this time, President Kennedy was assassinated. E. began to imagine himself as the president as soon as he could get rid of Johnson. This fantasy was relinquished when his confused sexual identity had been brought out into the open and he could talk about it directly. He wondered whether incest was appropriate; whether people should not adopt Far Eastern religions of the orgiastic type. Once he began to see the incest motif, he became concerned with having to play the role of the sophisticated male. His fantasies included masturbation, fetishism, and a variety of techniques for creating heightened sexuality. E. then involved his family, in a ritualized way, to make them provide him with excitations. The process was devious, but he programmed the sequence. He would fail his father, in order to get his father to rebuke him; this reaction would give the child the right to break something, then to make his sister cry; his mother, in turn, would be called upon to behave in a masculine manner by intervening; finally, E. would be able to masturbate.

The analyst mentioned that the patient had a curious way of confusing and distorting any reality connected to hostility. He would read about crimes of violence or perversion and then justify them to his parents, using long sophistries. He would say, for example, "The only thing wrong with this is that it's against the law. We should have more realistic laws." He did this at about eleven years of age, hence it could hardly be interpreted as adolescent revolt.

The analyst then reported a dream which had preceded the incident that threw the boy into the panic state. The setting was like a Persian harem. He, a woman, and a man were dressed in pajamas, and he and the man were engaged in a life-and-death struggle. It was understood that one must kill the other. It seemed that the man would surely kill him, until the woman gave E. a magic sword and said, "This magic sword will protect you from being killed, because if you cut off his head, it will grow back again, but then he won't harm you any more." In the dream, E. did not want to cut off the man's head and tried to resist in a variety of ways. Finally, he did decapitate the man, but the head did not grow back. In other words, the woman seduced him into committing the murder. E. first associated the woman in the dream with his mother, but immediately withdrew this association and identified her as his sister. Then he was unable to decide whether it was his father or his sister whom he killed, or his mother or his sister who had egged him on to do it. The identities of the people in the dream were amorphous, except for his own. He was a victim of an omnipotence and a license that were thrust upon him deceitfully.

The analyst told the study group that at this point the father was sexually impotent, like the man in the dream. The analyst felt that both the dream and the act of forcing his sister to wear the T-shirt in the school play represented E.'s method of reversing roles.

The analyst concluded his presentation at this meeting with an additional bit of information about the pathology evident in the family. The parents appeared nude before the children and the children were permitted to be nude before the parents. Furthermore, there was a peculiar game involved with beds. Anyone could move to anyone else's bed: the mother might end up in bed with the boy; the boy could end up in bed with his sister; the sister could get into bed with both parents. They all used each other's bathrooms, also. The only one who did not participate in this game was the uncle, who slept at the apartment two nights a week. Although the game seemed chaotic, the analyst thought there was some system to it in relation to the fantasy of who was baby-sitting and who was home. The moves were made in the middle of the night. A family member would go to bed in one bed and wake up in another, then deny any knowledge of having made the change. The parents claimed that they changed beds in response to hearing a child in distress, but the analyst doubted that this was the whole truth.

At the next meeting of the study group, the members summarized their impressions of the material:

1. The magical quality of the omnipotent fantasies in a ten-year-old pointed to an ego disturbance.

2. The private world sounded like a schizophrenic creation, a defense against the impulse to destroy the real world and against the anxiety generated by these destructive impulses. The readiness of the ego to alter the perception of the real world in response to these destructive impulses resulted in a similar readiness to perceive the body as either male or female, whichever was more comfortable at the moment. The sexual organization must be described as undifferentiated.

3. The capacity to displace reality from the real world to the magical facilitated perversion, in which the fantasy became more cogent than the reality.

4. The boy exhibited the fluidity in the image of the external world that is characteristic of the pre-ambivalent phase of development.

5. The case presented both neurotic, treatable features and more bizarre, schizoid, megalomaniac features. The latter may be a defense against the former.

6. The possibility of great improvement exists. The boy's development may catch up with his chronologic age. Also, he may improve as a result of identification with his analyst.

7. The case illustrated the abandonment of reality that appears in both perversion and psychosis.

8. E. had great hostility to the object, in this case the sister.

9. The child's obsession with crimes of violence when he was

about eleven years old represented the normal tendency of a boy of that age to endow the penis with powerful destructive capacity.

10. The mother's seductiveness aroused the boy's murderous wishes toward his father.

11. Sexual desire was then displaced from the mother to the sister. In getting the sister to wear the T-shirt with the picture of the monster, he projected his hostility onto her; this was also a sexually stimulating image.

12. The patient felt his omnipotence would be violated if he thought he could be influenced; omnipotence always accompanies weakness and the need to control aggression.

13. The assertion of omnipotence required the survival of the object of aggression as a witness in order to inhibit the destructiveness. In other words, the omnipotence gave the child the feeling that he could kill but that he could also revive, an example of the tolerance of contradiction that is so often seen in cases of perversion.

14. As a result of the patient's feeling of omnipotence, he could assign gender and anatomy as he wished and used this capacity to defend against castration fears, but the defense was not internalized.

15. The precursor of the castration fear was the fear of collapse as the result of separation from the mother's breasts. The omnipotence denied that, too.

The analyst then reported that mysteriousness and ambiguity about reality are actually continuing leitmotifs in this family. He suspected that the uncle's autobiography has been suppressed by the family. The boy cannot understand why the parents are ashamed of the uncle.

The analyst also learned that for two years the parents omitted to mention that the children had been sleeping in the same room for long periods of time. Apparently the parents were not always candid with the analyst, whether consciously or unconsciously, until suddenly there would be a breakthrough and they would reveal material from the past. The analyst had just learned, for example, that for many years the father and son had been involved in a game of mutual taunting; the game would end when one person lost his temper. The father restrained his temper but became more and more furious inwardly; he lost his temper vicariously through his son, when he got the son so angry that he threw something. Thus the boy would lose the game.

The father reported an incident that had happened months before in which E., on arriving home, saw a sick girl about twelve years old being carried out of the apartment house lobby on a stretcher. His father was supervising the scene. The father was very mysterious about it and refused to tell his son what had happened. He stood at the window and watched the girl being taken away by her doctor. The boy became more and more angry until finally he said, "Dad, if you don't talk to me I'm going to lose my temper." Whereupon the father said, "I am so proud of the way you acted, so proud of how mature you are now. I had to take care of this scene; I am responsible for this; now I am supervising it. You know I am doing my job; I bet you are proud of your father for doing his job." And the son responded: "Damn it all, isn't it your job to listen to your son? Here I don't know what's going on; I am worried. You got that kid taken care of, but what about me?"

In this curious but consistent pattern, the parents had been faithful about reporting ordinary things, but usually delayed reporting important things.

A member of the study group commented that this was an erotized sort of interplay. The one having the temper tantrum was the loser; if he could hold back, he became the winner. It was comparable to maintaining constant sexual excitement by teasing, short of ejaculation. Ejaculation meant loss of masculinity. The player who could hold onto the semen or sustain the excitement without orgasm (i.e. without losing his temper) could hold on to all the power.

The analyst reported that E. had recently been fascinated with religion, particularly with forms of Buddhism that prescribe a state of noninvolvement, in which one experiences without feeling and then eventually abandons the experience and identifies with the eternal. By now E. could talk about his fear of failing. He had progressed to the point when he could control the tantrums. He then realized that the tantrums represented the contest between himself and his father. These revelations illuminated a game that had been going on in the family for at least three years. The boy would go into his parents' bedroom at an unexpected moment in the night, trying to find his father in bed, but his father was always up when the boy entered the room. About two years before, the boy had had six months of massive insomnia. During that period, he wandered around the house, or stirred up the family in the middle of the night by looking for burglars. It finally became a contest: who would hear the burglar first—E. or his father?

There was an unspoken rule that if the boy woke up he was not to go into anyone else's room, but to knock quietly on the parents' bedroom door to let his father know he was awake. The father was supposed to come and sit on E.'s bed for three minutes and then leave. When E. reported this to the analyst, he said, "It isn't fair. Father wakes up before I hear the burglar and comes into my room, sits on my bed, stays longer than three minutes, goes back to his room, then is mad because I don't go to sleep and I go back and find that father is up. He is always one jump ahead of me, always."

A member of the study group commented that this game suggested a tradition of scientific detection, cops and robbers, cloak-and-dagger espionage; the preoccupation with the role of super-sleuth seemed itself to be libidinized.

The father corroborated that he always knew when the boy was having sleeping problems during that period. The father expressed himself in a characteristically bland way. One of the most frustrating factors in the boy's life was his father's imperturbability. While E. was having insomnia, his father kept requesting sleeping pills for himself, because his son's insomnia was keeping him awake.

The analyst interpreted this game as a pattern of competitiveness between the boy and the father and reported that the son set up, in fantasy, a similar competition between his father and the analyst.

E. reported a dream in which he was on a beach. A lifeguard was sitting on a high seat (suggesting spying) and someone was going to be drowned or lost. In the dream, the father neglected the son and the lifeguard had to save him. The son became furious because he had been saved; the father went off. Another element in the dream was not specifically identified with the lifeguard, but E. later coupled them in association. It was the name "Fixit." The boy said, "I see the word 'fixit' "; in association, he finally used the term "fixit-man," then "Mr. Fixit." Then he said, "Why does my father leave all the fathering to you?" The analyst asked the boy, "Does this make you mad at your father or at me also?" Negative transference material emerged. The boy said, in effect, "If you were not here, then he would have to do it himself."

A member of the study group asked whether the boy ever caught his mother in bed in these nocturnal wanderings, and the analyst replied that she was always in bed. The frustration, for him, in these night games, was that he always found his father standing silently by the window, as if nothing were going on. To the boy, this was a denial of activity between his father and mother. Further, it was a denial that his father was his father, or that his father had ever impregnated his mother.

E. recalled that his mother was always good to him, but that she did not understand him. The father understood everything but would not admit that he did, and left E. frustrated because he wouldn't express his understanding or say it in the way "the child" wanted it to be said. The analyst thought that the father competed with the mother for the mothering function and became symbiotic with the boy in the second year of the child's life. He thought the perversion was the outcome of literal seduction by the father at a pregenital age—not a genital seduction, but a seduction accomplished by replacing the mother in the maternal role. It is hard to say, however, whether the mother abdicated her role or whether the boy had an aversion to the mother that facilitated the father's competitiveness.

At this point the analyst summarized his understanding of the genesis of perversion. He thought that the family had both remarkable gifts and severe pathology. They wanted to retain both without admitting the pathology. Although there were distinguished people on both sides of the family, the parents were peculiarly modest about their gifts.

The boy was the first-born son of the only son of an immigrant who took a new and unusual anglicized name; no one else in the family bore that name. E. felt that he was involved in an information game: he seemed to take pleasure in testing the analyst's capacity to guess which of a number of eminent people were related to him by blood or marriage. The father played the game too. He was not satisfied to be simply a spy-counterspy; he played the mother role as well. In turn, his wife was willing to play both sides of the game. In effect, you couldn't tell a player without a program: players changed their costumes, everyone was playing all the roles.

Psychologically, the boy represented, for the father, the father's reactionary side. The father played the liberal but would not allow anything of his super-conservative background to be known; the boy became a radical right-winger and always represented the other side of the argument. The boy may have represented the father's ambivalence.

The analyst thought the boy dealt with all of this by developing mental and physical clumsiness as a façade. This façade permitted him to develop some hidden strength and to prepare to emerge from his cocoon. Eventually, perhaps with the help of the analysis, he was able to make his omnipotent fantasies somewhat syntonic with reality. In other words, the fantasies no longer involved supermen but ambitions he could talk about. These ambitions were competitive with the father's activities; he planned to outdo the father at his own game.

The relationship with the mother was so undercut that the analyst was not able to determine much about it. She claimed that the boy was always the perfect baby, but that meant nothing objectively to the analyst, because her definition of what was perfect had become so suspect. He thought by perfect that she probably meant whatever kept the boy's father quiet and satisfied. The analyst had no idea what actual mothering she did; it may all have been done by the nurse, who took care of the son from birth until he was about three years old. The nurse, then, might have been a good-mother image.

A member of the study group asked whether the two sides of the patient—the smart one and the stupid one—represented his identification with the abdicating mother, who was stupid, and with the alert father, so that the child never achieved any object constancy and therefore object representations were interchangeable.

The analyst, concurring, described one of the boy's fantasies: He walked into the surf and when the waves passed over him and he emerged, he was on a different planet and someone else had taken his place on earth, keeping the harmonies and the positions of the body in tune. It was an instantaneous, almost metaphysical switch, rebirth, and return. He would return instantly in the next wave, everything was reversible.

Another member of the study group remarked that he was unable to see the manifest perversion, which would presuppose sexual excitement. The analyst replied that E. did have sexual excitement, but it appeared only within the family. He masturbated, but he did not say that his fantasies were masturbation fantasies, although the analyst was sure they were.

His sex play with his sister included dressing up as a hermaphrodite, wearing breasts and a phallus, accentuating the penis and the breasts. In this play, he developed an erection. He also played a kind of superman vulture, frightening his sister so intensely that she had night terrors. He pretended he was a vampire and was going to drink her blood. He had conditioned her to respond to a signal: by saying one word, he could send her into a panic state.

Although the analyst knew that E. masturbated, the boy never talked about having ejaculations. The analyst attempted to get him to talk about it, but he could discuss ejaculation only in terms of expecting to have nocturnal emissions. The analyst inferred that E. inhibited ejaculation. He cited a dream in which the boy entered a room which was charged with electricity or atomic power. He knew that if he touched the button, the room would explode. Then he said, "No, it is not the room that is charged, it is the person who is charged, and they have the power within themselves, and if they touch the button, everything will explode." He then brought up associations about a future powering of the world by atomic power; about nuclear reactors; about the political uses of nuclear power; about the atomic bomb and the fear of losing control. The analyst speculated that the dream indicated that E. masturbated, but not to the point of ejaculation.

Another member of the study group offered another interpretation of the dream: that the concept that going into the room and touching the button would cause an explosion suggested that the relationship with the mother dominated the boy's unconscious fantasy life and filled it with erotic energies. He speculated that the boy then turned to the father in defense, overemphasizing the relationship with the father, as male homosexuals often do.

The analyst stated that the only material he had from the boy himself that indicated a need to flee from his mother was his association to the dream about the decapitation, and another item which was offered by the mother, and which the boy confirmed. He was a question-asker as well as a teaser. He demanded that she reiterate a certain formula, a compulsively outlined formula in which she said, in essence, "You can be a leader." It had to be said in a certain sequence, and in a certain manner. The associations to this the boy finally brought forth led essentially to the declaration, "You don't need to be tied to your mother's apron strings." In other words, "I hereby untie you."

A member of the study group suggested that this case involved a highly seductive mother and a passive, though less disturbed, father. In that case, it would inevitably be difficult for the boy to find his identification. He predicted, speculatively, that the boy never mentioned his penis in a literal way, and asked whether the boy could use the word.

The analyst acknowledged that he could use the word only when the analyst set the stage for it. The boy could not draw a human body, but he could name the parts of a body. In a sense, everything was free-floating and had to be hauled in by strings. In fact, the boy reported a dream in which the people were drifting out of the scene and he pulled them back with strings.

In a final comment, a member of the study group stated that he could easily visualize the genesis of the perversion in both parents' need to use the child quite literally to reconstitute their own deviant psycho-sexual development. As a result, the child was never able to reach the stage of ego development in which object, in terms of representation, was clearly delineated. That is why the boy was fixated on the modality of pre-logical thinking; every feeling he described was tied to a concrete visual object, and that is how little children talk. "Every child gets to know his body, in whole or in a partial sense, through the ministrations of the mother. If she cannot give respectful recognition to the body as a whole, to the function and to the parts, the child is also unable to achieve this recognition."

CASE IV

G. H., a fifty-two-year-old successful Wall Street investment counsellor, quite suddenly developed an acute perversion—a wish to be beaten. Alarmed by this impulse, which he recognized as perverse, he called the analyst who had treated him sixteen years earlier. On this occasion, he saw the analyst only seven times, at which point he reported that the symptom had disappeared completely and he discontinued treatment. The case was presented to the group primarily because, in the earlier analysis, there had been no indication of the existence of the wish or even of precursory fantasy leading to such a wish.

Mr. H. had originally presented himself for analysis for several reasons: he was unhappily married, suffered from general tension and uneasiness, and had severe feelings of inferiority. He was particularly bothered by one symptom of his anxiety—he perspired excessively during the day. His anxiety was fairly diffuse, although it intensified when he took airplane trips. He was a pilot himself, and his general anxiety about flying increased during his service in the airforce when he had to fly a superior from one place to another.

In that circumstance, his eyes watered so much that he could barely land the plane.

Although he was extremely handsome and had an unusually masculine build, he felt that his hips and buttocks were too large and found it painful to look at himself in the mirror. Upon entering analysis, he immediately developed a symptom—feeling ashamed of the analysis and wanting to keep it secret.

The patient's father and grandfather had both been wealthy men. The father was a hard-working businessman. He was strict with his children and though he rarely spanked them, he was severely punitive in other ways. For example, when the patient was about eleven years old, he shot out a window in the family's lakeside summer home. His father then took all his guns, broke them, and threw them into the lake. When the patient was younger, he had the habit of walking on tiptoe. His father threatened to cut his Achilles tendons if he continued.

The patient's mother was an accident-prone, hysterical hypochondriac, and her children were left to the care of nurses and governesses. When the patient was twelve years old he was sent to boarding school. The father was punitive toward the boy but was dominated by his wife, who exploited her illness.

An older brother, who was both athletic and intelligent, was the father's favorite. In contrast, G. was a plump, overweight, shy, and athletically inept child. When he was five years old, a younger brother was born and promptly became his mother's favorite, leaving the patient with an intense jealousy of both brothers.

The patient's social background threw some light on his ego structure. He came from a very wealthy set, most of whom were hedonistic and unintellectual. The patient differed from his peers in that he was ambitious and wanted to achieve on his own merit. Although he did not share the general behavior patterns of his peers, he was not really rebelling against their values. His goal was to become a successful businessman like his father.

In puberty G. grew slender and strong, and became interested in sports and socially successful. During this period, on an overnight train ride to boarding school, he was seduced by a classmate, and they indulged in mutual masturbation. This was his only homosexual experience. Soon after, he began to masturbate; his fantasies were of nude girls.

In the initial analysis, there was never any mention of beating fantasies. Occasionally he was stimulated when he happened to read about beatings in books. However, unlike individuals who are really stimulated by beating scenes and look for such accounts, the patient never sought out this type of literature. Dream material indicated that, when he was four or five years old, a maid or governess must have stimulated him sexually and permitted him to touch her breasts. Other than this, no significant sexual material appeared in his initial analysis.

When the patient was twenty-eight years old, his younger brother, who was also a pilot, was killed in a plane accident. The patient's first reaction was shock and some mourning, but the grief work did not seem adequate. Shortly afterward he developed what the analyst considered a counterphobic symptom—he increased his flying activities. His father had died ten years earlier and his reaction then also had been limited mourning.

Soon after the death of his younger brother, the patient fell in love with and married the daughter of a neighbor. His wife was a pretty but cold, restricted, emotionally impoverished person. He attempted to get warmth and affection from her, but she was rejecting and sexually frigid. At the beginning of his analysis, one daughter had been born and during treatment a second was born. When his wife was near delivery of the second child, the patient dreamed that his abdomen opened and a boy came out. (During the study group's discussion of the sudden onset of the perverse impulse, this dream was seen as significant.) The patient divorced his wife toward the end of his analysis.

The treatment could not be called a formal analysis because it was frequently interrupted by the patient's business trips. At its conclusion, he was symptom-free and self-confident and no longer felt the need to conceal the treatment. He had been moderately successful in a series of independent businesses.

Sixteen years later when the patient made his urgent call to the analyst requesting an appointment, he had been remarried and was approaching the seventh anniversary. His second wife, a divorcée with two sons, was a warm and loving person. The marriage contained an unusual degree of mutual understanding and functioned well sexually.

During the first session with the analyst, the patient did not mention the perverse symptom. Instead, he reported that his life had changed, that "the life influences seem to be with me." He felt that he had recently become increasingly productive and creative; however, he had had a recurrence of his old symptoms: uneasiness, tension, extreme perspiration under the arms. The symptoms did not seem to impede his functioning. He reported further that eight days before he contacted the analyst, he had had a sudden insight connected with the death of his younger brother. He realized that he had fallen in love with his first wife, whom he had known for years, only after he had seen her in physical circumstances that reproduced exactly those in which he had met his dead brother's fiancée. This insight gave him the curious feeling that he was leading a double life, or rather that he was a double person—himself and a continuation of his dead brother. In another session, he told the analyst that the day after he had had this insight, he developed a sudden urge to be beaten. After three days this drive became so compelling that he asked his wife to beat him. Although she was surprised by the request, she showed no aversion and complied.

The patient remained anxious after his initial hour with the analyst and continued to perspire, although he was able to conduct a business meeting successfully. It was after a business day that he felt the acute anxiety and fatigue, and required the beating in order to relax. During the fourth session he reported that these beatings had occurred four times a day. For example, he would lie nude on his bed when he came home from work and his wife would beat him on the buttocks with a brush or a slipper. Although the beatings were sexually exciting, the patient had no conscious fantasies during them and felt that they mainly relieved him from tension and anxiety. Usually, although not always, the beatings were followed by intercourse. Because he had never felt any such impulse before, he became so alarmed about this experience that he returned to the analyst.

It must be stressed, however, that he saw these visits not as a resumption of analysis, but as a brief treatment to overcome the perversion.

He went on to tell the analyst that three months previous to the onset of the urge, his wife had a hysterectomy. They attempted to have intercourse before the doctor gave permission for it, and he reacted by becoming temporarily impotent. However, they persisted, and he felt that his potency had not only increased but that he was at the peak of his masculine powers. He also reported that he had become aware of the contrast between his success and the relative failure of his once-admired and superior older brother. The patient, who in his childhood had occupied such an inferior position, had become the paterfamilias.

In a later session, the patient recalled that during puberty he had read a book about education in Sparta, in which the boys were whipped by virgins. Although he was sexually aroused at the time and probably masturbated, he did not read the book repeatedly. The analyst still felt that this perverse interest had not existed in his childhood or during puberty, or that it had been very fleeting.

The only other experience that was sexually unusual occurred after his divorce, during an affair with a very passionate woman who had stimulated his anus. After he broke up with her, he had for a time used a dowel for anal stimulation. Again, however, this was a brief experience which he did not require later in his sexual life.

The patient talked again about his recent business success. He also reported annoyance because the sweating intensified before the visits to the analyst—an obvious transference symptom. But he had no shame about the appointment, unlike the way he had felt in his initial analysis.

At this point, the patient's anxiety had lessened. Then the patient found a sketchbook containing his father's drawings, on the day before he came to the office for the sixth session. The patient studied it very carefully and become increasingly tense —tense enough to revive the need to be beaten. During the session, he recalled that he had sometimes watched boys being punished at boarding school. They were required to lie over a chair and receive three or four blows over the buttocks. Although this had never happened to him, he remembered that boys were permitted to watch this procedure and that he had been fascinated by it.

After this session, treatment was interrupted for four weeks because the analyst had to be away. When he saw the patient again, his tension had lessened, his symptoms had almost disappeared, and he no longer felt any urge to be beaten. He said he would not have come for this session if it were not for a dream he had had during the analyst's absence. Before describing the dream, he recounted an incident that occurred when his wife had her hysterectomy. Sitting in a sauna bath of a health club, he borrowed a long metal thermometer to check the temperature of the different levels of the sauna. He held it with a clasp, since it was too hot to touch. The thermometer slipped and fell onto his thigh, close to the genital area. Although he brushed it off immediately, it burned him, and a nasty, suppurating wound developed.

A few days before the seventh session, the patient had a dream in three parts. In the first, he looked at his thigh, which showed the scar. The scar then opened and exposed a festering wound reaching down to the bone. He could see the muscles and a lot of pus. Next to it was a completely circular imprint, like a healed scar. There were more ulcers down toward the knee. He said the dream seemed to have a military background. He showed the wound to many people and told them it might mean a military discharge. In the dream he used the word "military" instead of medical discharge, but it occurred to him later that a military discharge might also be gonorrhea, the *goutte militaire,* so it had something to do with an infection received as punishment for sexual activity. He associated the circular scar with another event, in which he had inserted a special lamp into Styrofoam to cool it and the Styrofoam had melted where the bulb touched it, so that a circular plug fell out.

In a second dream or in the second part of the same dream, a fully clothed man was lying in a bathtub, completely under water. When the patient entered, the man stood up and chatted with him.

The analyst associated this dream with rebirth and resurrection. He recalled that the patient's urge to be beaten was at its height during Easter week and that he had announced, at his first session, that he had felt that the "life influences seem to be with me."

In the third part of the dream the patient was at a large cocktail party. The entrance to the room was blocked by a table covered with flowers. As he went around the table, he met a grey-haired man. When he approached the man, the patient fainted and would have fallen on his back but the man caught him and broke the fall. He woke instantly. G. said he recognized the grey-haired man as his former father-in-law, whom he loved very dearly. He also associated the man with the analyst.

The day after the dream, he went through a very strange ego regression. He is left-handed, and in the course of writing a telegram, he noticed that he had written in mirror writing. He had not done mirror writing since he had learned to write at the age of six or seven years.

After this session, the patient left on a business trip. When he returned a few weeks later, he called the analyst to say that he was completely symptom-free and no longer needed treatment.

This case presented a unique characteristic in that nothing had been revealed in the course of the initial analysis that was a clear precursor to a masochistic perversion. Although the patient had an early interest in literary descriptions of beatings and had become excited when he saw the headmaster beat boys at school, the excitement was never highly cathected. The compelling question, then, was why did the perverse wish arise and why did it erupt in the need for action, rather than remain merely a fantasy?

The analyst speculated that the patient's rather sudden growth and success—combined with his older brother's decline and the growing awareness of his own hostility toward his father and his dead brother—created so much guilt that a relieving mechanism was required to counteract it. The mechanism chosen was a perverse one.

The study group agreed that unless the patient returned for further work, the data were insufficient to yield any clear-cut conclusions. The members did, however, speculate at some length about the possible genesis and dynamics in this case. In an early discussion, the following suggestions were made:

1. The beating represented an infantile and erotized punishment for superseding the father and brothers or for prohibited sexual activity.

2. The beating represented a masochistic wish to identify with a castrated woman because the patient retained a childhood feminine self-image both because of his prepuberal body build and because of his identification with his sick mother.

3. The beating generated sexual excitement which revived flagging potency.

4. The beating reproduced a meaningful infantile experience, which could only be inferred.

5. The beating was a defensive inversion of a wish to attack the woman sadistically.

The analyst himself saw the perverse act as also having significance as a rebirth or resurrection experience. He pointed out that the impulse and its acting-out occurred around Easter week. It followed an insight about the patient's first marriage that suggests that he felt guilt about the death of his younger brother. The patient may have seen his business success as an attack against his older brother, who was his father's favorite and whose life was, by contrast, a succession of failures. He could not accept his success as the product of his own effort but instead saw something magical ("The life influences seem to be with me"), and developed strong guilt feelings toward all the males in his childhood, father and brothers. In a sense, his personal success made him feel like a "triple murderer." In addition, his attempts to have intercourse with his wife too soon after her hysterectomy, before her doctor had given permission, produced guilt and anxiety. The analyst felt the patient saw these attempts as an effort to mutilate his wife. When his wife responded with warmth and love, he became impotent. When he regained potency and performed with what he saw as the highest degree of masculinity in his life, he then felt the need to be punished and possibly to assume the woman's role, in expiation for functioning as a successful male and thereby defeating (murdering) his father and brothers. The analyst therefore felt that the perverse impulse arose out of the need to alleviate intense anxiety and guilt. The patient himself had stated that he believed the beating had this function. The beating on the buttocks corresponds to the slapping of the buttocks of the newborn to promote breathing.

The group speculated that the hysterectomy may have been a triggering circumstance in that it removed any possibility for the patient to have a son. Both his former and present wives had sons, but he had only daughters. The group suggested that this may have produced anger, which triggered the anxiety and guilt that led to the perverse impulse. One member of the group suggested that he would classify this perversion as a neurotic perversion rather than an impulse-satisfying perversion; in other words, that it was more a neurotic symptom than an instinctually channeled form of libido gratification—a formulation that seemed supported by the patient's recognition that he needed the beating as a defense against his guilt feelings.

One further speculation by the group was that the first analysis had never been totally completed, in that the patient had always identified the analyst with his father, as his anxiety and excessive sweating during the analytic hours would suggest. They speculated further that his return to the analyst when he was frightened by this impulse which he recognized as perverse might also have been an attempt to get the analyst to assume the beating role and complete the father identification.

The group speculated that the concatenation of events: the absolution by the father-analyst figure, the fact that he did not injure his wife by attempting to have intercourse with her prematurely, and his business and sexual success—all following upon his insight that he felt that he was a triple murderer—may have given rise to the rebirth fantasy. The analyst felt that this speculation was supported by the curious fact that this man of fifty-two years still looked as young as he had sixteen years earlier, suggesting that he still felt himself young and ineffective. If these feelings did exist, they would help to explain why he saw his success as a magical event rather than a result of his own achievements.

Because the patient did not return to explore further the meaning of his perverse impulse, the group felt that he was in flight from additional insight. They agreed that any interpretations they might make were of necessity purely speculative and therefore the complete discussion has not been included here.

CASE V

I. J., an attractive, extremely intelligent, twenty-year-old white male, was referred for psychiatric evaluation by the health service of the college he attended because he had been cutting classes and was consistently on probation. The first psychiatrist who saw him referred him to the psychoanalyst who presented this case to the group.

I. was one of three children: he had an older brother, who was athletic, popular, and generally successful, and had a younger sister, an athletic and apparently aggressive girl, whom he disliked intensely. The mother was described to the analyst by the referring psychiatrist as a perfectionist.

The patient's family lived in a Midwestern city where they owned a successful advertising business. I. himself was a tall, attractive, rather boyish young man with blonde hair and a light complexion. He was interested in literature, but his taste, he said, changed constantly. "I love poetry but I cannot do anything about it. I like to write but I never do."

The analyst held two preliminary consultations before deceding to accept the patient.

At the second consultation, I. saw another young man leaving, whom he recognized as a student at the same college he attended. When the analyst asked him how he reacted to this, he replied, "I was jealous," indicating that a positive transference already existed. At this session he stated that his main concern was homosexuality. He "had a long history of homosexuality, not in acts, but in concern." He described a seduction by a counsellor at a summer camp. This seduction occurred when I. was fourteen or fifteen years old. He revealed little about the incident, except to call it a seduction. In the consultation sessions he never volunteered details about "loaded" material, nor could they be elicited.

A year ago (age nineteen), I. had picked up a man in the city, and they had engaged in mutual masturbation. Again, his description of the incident did not reveal what had actually gone on. He complained that there was no closeness in his social life, that he was afraid of girls, and that they made him nervous. He slept a great deal, neglected his work, and he was now on probation for the third time.

Another preoccupation mentioned in the consultation hours was the conviction that he had a smaller penis than other boys.

The first analytic hour following the consultation sessions, I.'s initial comment was: "I dislike this napkin you have on this pillow. I cannot stand people who protect their furniture."

Very soon the patient began to center completely on the analyst and his private life, saying, "I wonder, do you have a wife, or is she dead? I have never seen her. Why are your rooms so orderly? My friend said it is a sign of compulsive character if somebody has such an orderly room."

He reported a dream. "I was with a counsellor at summer camp. He was discussing the draft deferments with me. He was the one who made passes at me." (The analyst's unstated interpretation of this first dream: "You [the patient] wonder whether I am a homosexual. Have I a wife? Is she dead, etc. Have I a wife or will I make passes at you?")

The patient then talked about a party he was to attend that night. "There is the friend I became friends with so quickly at college. Now he doesn't want to room with me next year. We will meet tonight and we will smoke pot." The analyst was silent. I. said, "Well, what do you think?" The analyst: "Why do you need to know what I think?" The patient: "I am going to be a father just like you are." (That is, he too is going to treat his son in a non-punitive way.) The positive transference, which developed almost from the first moment, was becoming a serious obstacle to analytic work.

At that time the analyst was told by the referring psychiatrist that I.'s father had sent him a summary statement of the bills for the doctor to verify for tax purposes, and that the father had over-stated the amount of the bill. The analyst and the referring psychiatrist speculated that this might indicate some psychopathic trend in the father.

The patient reported that one relative was an alcoholic and that another drank constantly but was never drunk. His father drank moderately. I. seemed to be trying to explore all the abnormality in his family. His main concern, however, was: "What is my father like?"

He said, "As a little boy I always wanted to be a girl. I played with girls. Not with my sister, she was younger. I dressed in girl's clothes; not in my sister's—my mother would never have allowed that. I found clothes in a trunk in the attic and dressed up and did girls' impersonations." "At times," he said, "I played with my sister, using chairs, and so on, to build caves and tunnels. I liked to wear a bathrobe, go to the toilet, and lift the robe like girls lift their skirts in sitting down. I envied girls. I was never athletic. I always saw boys playing baseball on a nearby lawn from my window. My brother was better in athletics, in baseball and in games."

At this point in analysis, the analyst had to cancel an hour. Following the cancellation, I. missed two hours. The analyst telephoned after the second missed session, and I. appeared for the next two sessions. When I. reappeared, he did not explain why he missed his sessions. He merely said, "I just didn't feel like it." He then reported that he had gone to a party at his great-aunt's on the evening of the day the analyst had cancelled. Two young women were present, and he disliked them. He felt like an outsider, and drank too much. He made a mental note to go out after the party and pick up a man. He went downtown at midnight, saw a young man leaning against a building, and asked him what he was doing. The young man invited him to his room. During this conversation, I. thought he might be robbed, but he went anyway. He had, he claimed, no sexual intentions, no sexual desires, but he felt adventurous and had a feeling of "what the hell." When he entered the room another man stepped out of the closet. The two took his money, then sent him away. He was, he claimed, merely amused by the experience.

The analyst pointed out to the patient that this happened after the analyst had "left" him. He then remarked on the analyst's accent. He said, "I wonder, do you speak French to your wife?" He went on to mention that his family had employed a French-born maid for twenty years and that the woman who took care of the children when they were small also spoke French.

I. then changed the subject to comment that the analyst's books looked terribly boring, and he thought the analyst had never read them. He then reported a two-part dream which followed his seeing the film, "Dracula." He had originally seen the film when he was ten years old, and had had a terrible nightmare afterward.

The first dream: "I was back at summer camp. None of the boys knew me. They looked at me while I walked through the building. I met the counsellor. He greeted me, and everybody noticed that he knew me well. He smiled at me and said 'You are a good boy.' "

He continued, "In the second dream there was a girl, or was it a woman? It was a terrible and an awful dream. She was a sadist. But then there was a part of her that was very nice. It is confusing. I can't explain it. There was a long board with many compartments, each having a cover. You lifted up the cover and what came out was either good or awful."

I. then talked about his mother a great deal, saying that she constantly complained about him but always wanted to have him around. She always gave him advice and could never leave him alone.

The next hour was full of resistance. "Why should I play this game (analysis) to your rules (free association)? What's the use of asking you questions about your room, about you, etc., if you don't answer?" He had a coughing fit and sat up: "Oh, I won't look at you." The analyst replied, "But that's why you sat up, because I don't answer." The analyst then asked him to lie down to analyze his "what's the use" feeling about analysis.

The analyst felt that I. had reported the dream in order to

follow the analytic rules to say something, to be a good boy, expecting that the analyst would then return the gift and tell him about himself. When the analyst failed to do so, the resistance arose; namely, "What's the use of telling you anything? You never tell me anything. That's the rule." I. then mentioned that while he lay on the couch he had a compulsive smile on his face. He couldn't get it off, and he had that smile whenever the analyst spoke. The analyst had never noticed the smile.

The analyst asked him, "Tell me about the counsellor and what happened." I. replied, "Oh, that's a long, long story." Then: "Oh well, I might as well tell you."

"He lay down in bed with me, and we tickled each other on the stomach. I found it sexually exciting and pleasurable. We laughed and we talked (the smile, the grinning in the analysis)—no genital contact or genital play." The analyst inferred that repression was operating. He asked I. whether the counsellor had had an erection. The patient insisted, "No. No. This was just lying together, tickling, talking, and laughing. Later I didn't like him. I didn't like him because he preferred other boys."

After this session the patient missed the next hour. When he arrived for the following session, he said he had been up all night writing a paper. He commented that he had taken a course about Erikson's "autocosmic play." The correct term, of course, is microcosmic." The analyst pointed out that "autocosmic" sounded like "autoerotic." The patient followed the idea very nicely: "It would be cool to hug a vacuum cleaner and see what your parents think." In other words, he retreated from the animate object. He continued to ask questions about the analyst: "Do you look at your art books? Who selected the slipcovers? Who selected the upholstery? You selected the upholstery. Your wife selected the slipcovers. And I think about you going to the park. I like to walk on a day like this." He showed the analyst a ring he was wearing—three rings woven into one. He had wanted to buy it for three weeks. He moved it up and down on his finger and said "It's like masturbating."

He became impatient again. "Why don't you tell me whether you have a wife? Maybe she's dead. It's not nice for you if I talk about her and she is really dead. I wonder about your wife. I think you both go to the theatre together and you both go to the park together. I thought of visiting you in the country this summer." A pause. Then, "There's something very strange in our being in this room alone. There's noise upstairs. This could be your wife."

At the following session, I. told the analyst he would not be in the next week. "I am going to New York to visit my brother." It was the end of examination time and the dorms were to be closed. He had no place to go except to one apartment, terribly ugly and ten blocks from the college. He felt hurt at being offered no other option and would rather go away than compromise. He planned to go home for the weekend. The father was in London on business. The mother told him over the telephone that if he did not get a haircut, he might just as well not come home. He asked the analyst, "Well, what shall I do?" (He always attempted to get the analyst to make decisions for him.) "If it were your son, what would you do?" Analyst and patient discussed the battles I. always had with his mother. The mother said, "You would look like such a nice young boy if your hair were cut." He said, "No, I will not cut it, and I will go home." Actually, the patient's hair was not excessively long. He was a very neat boy with good taste.

The analyst pointed out that he would keep I.'s hours open for him and charge for missed appointments. I. responded, "Well, I know that," and immediately returned to his displeasure at not being told anything about the analyst's personal life. The session ended with the understanding that I. would return after the week's absence. However, I. did not appear when expected; after he missed two appointments, the analyst called the parents' home. I. was there, and his parents did not know he had had appointments. When he returned for his next session, he commented, "Of course, now when the bill comes there will be a row; I never think what lies ahead." He continued, "I don't want to talk. I never open my mail—I know what is in it is awful. I never add up my checks, either. I never write them down in the stubs."

The analyst: "So you don't want to talk about your thoughts because they are going to be awful things?" The analyst pointed out that I.'s father would realize, when he saw the bill that I. had missed appointments. The patient replied, "Well, I am doing the same thing I do in college, just not going when I am expected."

The next session: "What is there to say?" Then he asked, "What did you think, when I told you about picking up a man and being robbed?" The analyst reminded him that the episode had never been analyzed and that it had occurred the night of the great-aunt's party—the day the analyst could not see him.

I.: "I am so pleased that you remember. Dr. 'X' (the referring psychiatrist) always forgot everything. (A pause.) Aren't you going to say anything to that?" Then he said, "What would you say if I told you that I had relations with a guy? Do you think it's good or bad?"

The analyst: "Well, I don't think in these terms."

I.: "That's what my mother would think, either good or bad. If you aren't good, it's just because you don't want to be. This is my mother's philosophy." He said he was thinking of picking up a man again. "The city is full of temptations. That's why I would like to live at the shore with a friend. I have nothing to do in the city, just come to analysis."

The analyst asked him about his thoughts and his fantasies about picking up a man and having relations. He couldn't answer. The analyst still knew little about his actual homosexual practices and wishes.

At the next session, he arrived five minutes before the end of the session. He had gone to the barber to get a haircut and a hair wash, and it had taken longer than he expected; he took the wrong bus. He said, "The funny thing is, today I wanted to talk to you." He recognized the ambivalence in wanting to talk but not keeping his appointment. The analyst learned that Paul had picked up a man the night before.

The last week before summer vacation, I. was scheduled for five sessions. He arrived twenty-five minutes late for the first. He was silent. Then he said, "I read in a Catholic paper about the movies they forbid to be seen. It's ridiculous." The analyst: "What is it I apparently forbid you to see and consider bad to do?" He finally answered directly: "Last Thursday night I went and picked up a man at his apartment. He was thirty-six years old." The analyst reminded him of the session in which he had almost warned that if he could not get the analyst to talk about himself and reveal personal information, he would go and pick up a man. This structured, sequential interpretation, pointing out relationships, was somewhat tutorial, for I. still needed tutoring about what the process of analysis is.

The next day he was on time. First question: "Is the layout of your apartment upstairs the same as on this floor? Do you have a wife? Does she have to stay upstairs all day?" (The analyst reminded him of what they had already recognized—that I. saw the situation as "a wife versus homosexuality.") Then he informed the analyst that he was disappointed because he would be continued on probation. He had received one A, two Cs, one D and one F. The F was in Physical Education. He admitted that for two semesters he was unable to go to the locker rooms or to the showers. "Playing tennis is OK—after that, I can go to my room." He was fearful of being conspicuous by not taking a shower when in gym—afraid that the other students would "draw conclusions"—so he didn't attend. Furthermore, he had decided he did not want to continue in college. He didn't go to his art classes either, although he got a B in sketching. He did well but he was very irregular. He said that he liked that course and he did not understand why he didn't even do things he liked to do. "I just ignore classes. I don't do anything."

At the next session, I. related that he sat in the park the previous night. He saw all these sex-hungry men go by and look at him. He found it revolting. A man sat down next to him, propositioned him, and I. told him he wasn't interested. This man talked to him. He was married. He was unhappy. It was sad and pathetic. "That a married man should look for homosexual contact. I felt superior to them, and I enjoyed rejecting them." Then he said, "The counsellor at summer camp had the same look in his eyes, a hungry, sexy look, even in the photograph in the yearbook." The analyst and patient talked about the counsellor again, and again I. insisted that there had been no genital play or contact. He wondered why neither his father nor his mother did anything about this counsellor. "They must have known." (The analyst interpreted privately: "My father threw me to a homosexual counsellor, taking some secret delight in my homosexual experience.") He told about another counsellor from the same camp who invited a boy into his apartment. The boy reported the counsellor, who was then dismissed. I. never reported anything to anybody. When asked why, he said, "Well, simply not to implicate myself."

During the next hour, I. reported that his father had called and was furious, worried, defeated, and scolding. What emerged from this session was that the incident of the referring psychiatrist's bill, which the father had presumably overstated for tax purposes, had been misinterpreted by both the referring psychiatrist and the analyst. I. had simply told his father that the bill was higher than it was in fact, and had not only pocketed that difference but had failed to pay the full bill. On the telephone his father had blown up and told him, "You take a job next year. No support from me except for your analytic bill." This threat was frightening, and I. was frightened. All he could say to his father was, "I miscalculated in my checkbook." Of course this excuse infuriated the father even more. I. admitted to the analyst that he knew all along what he was doing. Then he said, "Why doesn't my father trust me anyway? When I say I miscalculated, why doesn't my father believe me? He should have believed me."

The analyst then asked, "Could you pay back this money from your summer job?" I. replied that he saw no reason to suggest that and wouldn't do it unless his father demanded it. I. then asked the analyst to talk to his father about his bill and the question of job versus college for the following year. The analyst at first refused and explained that he did not take a mediating role. This was not the function of an analyst. Then he changed his mind, feeling that the consequences of the father's ultimatum might be disastrous. He insisted that if he talked to I.'s father, I. must be present. He agreed. He commented, "I could never talk to my father in my whole life."

I. was aware that, with the next bill from the analyst, his father would detect his new delinquency, his absence for two weeks; he wanted the analyst to tell his father about this in advance. The analyst agreed to a telephone call because of his feeling that the father's either/or ultimatum might be disastrous. He believed that I. was unable to hold a job at that time.

It was agreed that he would telephone I.'s father on the following day, when I. knew his father would be at home. But he did not appear for the session. The next day, when he came on time, he claimed that he had gone to the beach, gotten lost driving home, and arrived at the analyst's door five minutes before the end of the hour. He had then decided that it was not worthwhile coming up. The analyst thought this excuse was probably a lie.

I. remained in the room while the analyst telephoned his father. The analyst explained to his father that the discipline he was proposing—the job, no college, no money, except for the analyst—would probably fail; that I.'s delinquent behaviour was of long standing and would not suddenly disappear. The analyst also told his father about the two week's absence, describing it as another example of the pattern of delinquency, and explained that he was alerting the father to this in advance partly to express his certainty that this behavior was part of his son's illness. I. was pleased to listen to the analyst's end of the conversation. He felt the terms the analyst used were justified and had no objection to being so described.

At the next session, the patient mentioned that whenever his mother approved of something he wanted and liked to do, he became embarrassed and dropped the activity. At this point the analyst interpreted his failure to keep his appointment earlier in the week as an example of not doing what he liked to do, what his mother wanted him to do, and what the analyst wanted him to do in terms of an intimacy, of a meeting of minds. He wanted the analysis, his mother wanted it, the analyst wanted it, and thus analysis became embarrassing. He responded, "My mother sees everything in black and white and as long as you do what she wants, it's good." He then talked about a summer course for which he had enrolled at a school in his home city. When his mother asked him how it was going, he said, "Well I finally get it, what chemistry is all about." In reality he had gone to only one class. He had then retired to his room to "study," feeling a combination of guilt and glee.

The patient switched to talking about his sister, then immediately returned to discussing his mother and the fact that she used him as an informant. "She always wishes to hear the worst."

At the next session he talked about what to do in the fall. He did not want to return to college and suggested art school. The analyst did not support this suggestion, feeling it would be the same thing as college, but more loosely structured. He then talked about his fears that he was unable to pass science, math, or languages. He would like to stay on in the apartment in which he was then living, the ugly apartment to which he had objected earlier, but his father felt the apartment would be too expensive. The session ended with the conclusion that I. should have a reduced college program, and perhaps an evening art class at an art school.

At the next session he came from a museum at which he had seen a Gauguin and Kandinsky show. "It was intolerable. People were talking nonsense." He went on to say that he was envious and got jealous because Gauguin's work is exactly what he wanted to do. He asked the analyst, "Do you ever look at your art books?"

The analyst: "Why do you ask?"

I.: "My parents never do. I gave them a beautiful book about Byzantine art and they've never even opened it. They like nothing I like. They don't understand me at all. We cannot talk to each other. I got a letter from my mother, and I was surprised there was not a word about the bill in it."

The bill had been paid without comment. At the session, I. was on time. He told the analyst, "Well, I sent on your bill." (Pause.) "There is nothing to say today." (Pause.) "Do you have a word of good advice for me?" The analyst: "Well, I think you've had enough of that in your life." I: "My mother never said goodbye to me without giving me tons of good advice." The analyst: "And I do just the opposite."

I. then launched into a discussion of the family life to which he would be returning the following day. "My father asked me to select pictures for his newly decorated den. He won't object to my choice because he doesn't understand pictures anyway. We never sit around in our family and talk, never. My sister will be there all summer. She's unbearable. She believes in keeping in good physical condition. Is that normal for a girl? She plays games—tennis—to compete. She hits the ball so hard, and she complains if you make an error; it's no fun to play with her." Then, "It's too bad that we can't go on with the analysis." When the analyst responded with verbalization about his leaving for vacation, about loss and separation, I. asked "Are you making fun of me?"

The analyst received one long letter from him during the summer. He wrote: "I am still frightfully bothered by my seemingly chronic homosexual desires. I really don't want to react the way I do, but I don't seem to be able to control it. I don't even want to have to control it. I look at a young boy with a good physique and immediately think about going to bed with him. When I masturbate, my fantasies are always homosexual. This really is ridiculous writing. I am really surprised by the fact that I haven't had any incidents recently. I have to tell you about a lot of things when I see you. It all seems too simple and artificial when I write them." Nevertheless, he never described his homosexual fantasies.

When he returned in the fall, his first words to the analyst were: "I think about the summer you had, and I imagine that your son was with you." The analyst pointed out that this was always his fantasy—to be with the analyst as his son; to have an understanding and loving father.

The trip from the Midwestern city in which he lived to the city in which he attended college was made by the patient and his parents. En route, they had to share a room. He talked in the analytic session about people who talk in their sleep. The analyst: "Do you?" I.: "Yes, I do." The analyst, "Did you do that last night?" I.: "Yes, I did. My parents told me I did." It was clear that I. had a fear of sleeping in a room with anyone because of his fear of saying anything. His parents told him that he had said, " 'It had to be fixed on the bottom side, no, on the bottom edge.' I also said something about my father's brother-in-law. I like him. I dream a lot but I never remember anything. It was the same last night." The analyst made no interpretation.

At the next session, however, I. began by describing a film in which a girl was talking about an analyst to whom she told only what she wanted him to know. The analyst commented, "Well, you did the same yesterday during your hour." I. replied, "Do you mean about the dream?" The analyst: "Yes." I.: "All right. I don't want to tell you, but anyway I will." He was referring to the previous session, when he had claimed that he never remembered dreams.

He described the dream. "The dream was very interesting; a friend of mine was in the dream—I don't know what our relationship is—do you know what Vienna sausages are? They are like frankfurters but cut off at either end; they are also short, not fat, like a finger." In the dream his friend showed him his penis; it was a Vienna sausagelike penis changed to a spike, with a sharp point like an antelope horn, as thin as a pencil. "He unzipped, or something, and then it got big. We had some kind of homosexual relations, but I don't know what kind. I also had another dream last night, it was a picture of men's bodies. They had no heads, that means the heads were out of the picture; extremely masculine, muscles everywhere. They were in funny positions, distorted, with huge genitals; all the figures were packed together. They were covered with something like stockings, very much smooth over the surface of the body but the muscles showed, like Michelangelo's slaves struggling. I didn't see any heads. Everybody was impressed by these bodies and genitals. An exercise class started. It was muscle building. Twenty people wanted to get huge genitals." After describing the dream, the patient said, "I wince when I talk about it. I hate it." There was a silence.

The analyst asked him what he hated. He replied, "What? I don't want to tell you." The analyst referred back to the previous session in which he had indicated so clearly that he did not want to tell anything. He asked what had to be fixed on the bottom side.

I. then said, "My genitals are too small. The dream was pleasant but the Vienna sausages were horrible, like mutilated and skinned." When the analyst related this to his homosexual practice, of taking the penis in his mouth, I. said, "Well, there is a mask of fear." He did not exclude the interpretation.

Having then, in a sense, dared to talk about himself too much, I. reverted to his original techniques for flight: the dreams had come too close to his fantasies, and he returned to asking the analyst personal questions about himself. Once again he argued that there was no point to his associating if the analyst told him nothing about himself.

From this point on in the study group meetings, the presenting analyst no longer detailed the case session by session. Instead, he selected revealing and relevant incidents that occurred in the sessions preceding the group's meetings. He told the group that I.'s difficulty in talking arose not only from his unwillingness to reveal anything about his own activities and fantasies but also from his blank mind. I. frequently said, "Nothing is on my mind, nothing." Although he never fell asleep on the couch, he had begun to sleep more and more at home.

Technically he was still a student, but he no longer attended classes. Since he was on probation, these cuts meant that he would be dropped by the college. He and the analyst talked about his applying for a leave of absence and looking into art schools, because he was really interested in art and design. But I. was reluctant to do this because he felt that, if he did start something he liked, he would not carry it through.

His day-to-day existence became increasingly passive. He listened to music, made himself tea, got his laundry done. He wore a fresh shirt every day and was always meticulously dressed.

In one session, I. complained that he really knew no one and was not known by anyone, that he was terribly alone. He felt he constantly had to hide. As the analysis proceeded, he eliminated everything from his life except his contact with the analyst.

The patient and the analyst agreed that when I. stayed away, either the analyst would call him or he would call the analyst. He called just ten minutes before one session and said, "I won't be in today. I don't feel like it."

The analyst replied, "Come anyway."

I. said, "Why should I? I have nothing to say."

The analyst: "Well, let us see. Take a cab and come over."

In ten minutes he arrived. He mentioned that he had read the analyst's article. The analyst asked him, "What do you remember? What struck you in the article?" He replied, "The girl who is dressed up like a boy."

The analyst: "That is the opposite of what you did." I. then mentioned that his cousin told him that he used to dress up in her clothes. This contradicted what he had said in one of the early sessions when he stressed that he dressed only in girls' clothes that he had found in the attic. When the analyst pointed this out, I. said he did not remember but felt since his cousin said it happened, there must have been some truth in it. I. went on to tell the analyst that he played with dolls up to the sixth grade. He also described having bought an eyelash curler when he was in junior high school and, another time, having put foundation lotion on his cheeks. He said the girls in school asked him if he powdered himself. He used an eyebrow pencil, but so lightly that no one could see it. In other sessions he mentioned that his mother had accused him of being vain. "But," I. said, "she really is vain. She says my father is vain, that he spends too much time in front of the mirror. That's not true. I spend lots of time in front of the mirror."

I. also described memories of liking to look into people's drawers—into his mother's dresser drawer where she kept all sorts of things, not her clothes.

From time to time, in the course of three hours in which he reluctantly gave the analyst meagre bits of information, he wrote his father that he was having a rough time in analysis. He constantly tried to establish an intimacy with the father who did not understand him.

At one session I. arrived and said, after a long silence (the analyst now allowed silences to continue longer and longer), "What should I do? This is the deadest place I know. All these books mean absolutely nothing to me. Everything is so orderly here. Nothing ever moves. Everything is dead. I think of a bunch of bananas, peeled, and I take a picture of them. And then it stops again. This room is so stagnant. Even the pictures are dead except the drawing that hangs over your chair." In actuality, this was the one picture in the room I. could not see.

The analyst pointed out to I. that what he was saying was that the only thing in the room that was alive was sitting right under that picture, namely, the analyst. I. then talked about his father and mentioned that his father liked the photographs he had made for his den. Then he began to talk about his home—now the dead place was the home.

I.: "No one in my family ever says anything. My mother likes everyone. She never has any criticism to make. What my parents say means nothing. It is false and has no meaning. How can praise from them mean anything if I know they don't feel anything? The principle is to be nice to your children, but they don't care enough to be critical. I don't understand them. My father is like pictures that tell a story. I can't understand them." The analyst then asked him, "Did you decorate your father's den with pictures?" (This was a reference to something I. had told him before the summer vacation, when he had been so pleased at his father's willingness to allow him to decorate his den.) I. again was startled. He said, "How did you know?" The analyst reminded him that he had talked about it before the summer. I.'s response was, "I feel extremely happy."

This, too, was a repetition of an incident in an earlier session, when he had been so pleased and surprised because the analyst remembered something he had said earlier. Again he contrasted the analyst to the referring psychiatrist, describing him as someone who forgot everything and who told the patient everything about himself, about his family and his children, his country house, everything. I. mentioned that he appreciated the fact that the analyst did not do the same thing, yet he couldn't stand it.

The analyst described another session in which I. talked about having gone to gym to play ball and again having refused to shower. The analyst asked him if his reluctance was from fear that he might become sexually excited in the company of the other men, or whether it was because he was ashamed of being seen because of having a small penis. He answered without hesitation: "I am ashamed of being seen." He paused and then continued, "I like to be nice to myself. I love to buy things. I love to spend money, but then I lose interest gradually and this leads to always wanting extras."

I. was known in the family as someone who always wanted something extra, something that was not being served. The analyst interpreted this trait as the reverse of what he really felt; namely, that he had been disadvantaged by nature or by his mother, that he did not have a good penis like his brother, and that the world owed him something. I. laughed. The analyst: "Is it funny?" I.: "Yes, it sounds funny when you say it." Then he became serious and said, "Because I became aware of my small penis when I was fourteen years old."

In the next hour he made interesting remarks. He had gone to the bathroom in the analyst's office after the previous hour and he told the analyst, "I had the thought that you might catch me there. I know what you do if I go to the toilet before the hour—you come out at the time and ask me in; but I don't know what you do after the hour." Then he talked about his interest in meeting the other patients coming in. Although he tried to avoid them, he was curious and jealous.

In another hour, I. was smiling and finally admitted that he would really like to ask the analyst to give him money. This occurred in the middle of the month, when the bill should have been paid by I.'s father. The analyst then asked him whether he had sent the bill to his father and I. admitted that he had not, but explained that he didn't want to write the letter. The analyst was aware of, but did not point out, the fantasy that withholding the money would permit I. to control the analyst.

I. missed an hour and called the analyst, who asked him to come. He arrived about fifteen minutes late. The analyst asked him: "Is there any obvious reason why you didn't want to come today?" He replied, "Yes, I am going to meet a fellow tonight in a bar. I made a date. How can I come here and tell you what I do if you do not want me to do this? I'm disgusted with myself for doing these things, and I don't want to tell you about it."

This admission led into a discussion of I.'s wish to please

others. He then asked the analyst about the date. "What shall I do? Shall I go or shall I not go?"

At this point in the analytic process, it was possible for the analyst to interpret for him the meaning of I.'s wish to have the analyst tell him what to do. He pointed out that I. equated understanding with loving. Therefore, if the analyst were to say to him, "Don't see that man," I. would interpret it as meaning "stay with me; I want you for myself." The analyst went on to interpret many of I.'s actions as messages to the analyst that he loved him, and I. replied, "Well, I knew this all the time."

He then described going hunting with his father, who wanted him to handle a gun and hunt. He never did learn to handle a gun, but his brother did. Nevertheless, he was very proud when his father came to see him and always went with his father. He particularly liked to go into the woods with him, which had come out in the analysis as a wish to go into the park with the analyst and talk. In the session, the wish to be with the father suddenly changed and I. said, "I bought myself a cashmere sweater." Then he described it. "I love the softness. I like to be good to myself. It is so soft. I feel it, and I feel good." The analyst asked him who wore cashmere sweaters and I. replied, "Millions of people." But when the analyst persisted in asking precisely whom he remembered as wearing cashmere sweaters, he responded, "My mother."

The analyst did not interpret these associations until the following hour. Then he called his attention to the association between the cashmere sweater and his identification with his mother and soft skin. He further pointed out that I. had mentioned the sweater immediately after talking about being with his father and going hunting with him and his wish to be close to him. He suggested that I. believed that in order to obtain his father's love he had to be a girl. When the analyst developed this idea, I. responded by saying, "My mother always told me, 'You are too attached to your father,' but I always thought my problem was my mother."

The next session opened with the patient asking the analyst, "Are you my friend?" He said that he had heard that analysts should be friends of their patients and then said: no, he did not think the analyst was his friend because friends share confidences both ways. He asked the analyst whether he liked taking his dog out or considered it a chore. (This was interpreted as a reflection of his frequently expressed wish to go for a walk with the analyst in the park.) He continued, "I always look around when I go to a concert to see if I will see you." Then he talked about girls, saying he never dated and was very shy with girls. "When I am with girls—and there are a few that I know and visit—I am terribly nervous. I watch out not to be trapped and not to be taken in. I can't stand to be touched."

The analyst asked about I.'s application to art school, but I. had not filed it. After this question, the patient stopped talking. When the analyst asked him what he was thinking about, he said, "Nothing." After some silence, the analyst interpreted I.'s inability to speak as being a reflection of his fear of being trapped in art school, in the vagina, possibly in the vagina of his mother. He reacted to this with great agitation. He said, "If we talk about such horrible things, I won't come here any longer." But he then described a series of sadistic and aggressive films he had seen, in which women were the aggressors. He mentioned that he had started to buy all sorts of honey, a different kind every day. When the analyst asked him, "When did you eat honey?", the patient replied, "Oh, not for years and years. When I was little, my grandmother always had honey at breakfast."

The analyst then reported to the group a number of things that had emerged in previous sessions: for example, the analyst and the patient discussed how much I. behaved like his mother in his need to be clean and meticulous. The discussion occurred immediately after he had skipped an hour following a session in which the material had been, in I.'s words, "dirty." The analyst pointed out to him that what he was saying was that the analyst made him dirty. I. responded, "You know what I did during the hour I wasn't here? I cleaned." The theme of avoidance of dirt showed up in the mother's removing from her son's library all books she considered dirty, such as *Lady Chatterley's Lover*. In a sense, the analyst pointed out, he did exactly the same thing—he cleaned his apartment. In one session, to which he came immediately after having showered and put on a clean shirt, he wanted to sit up because lying down on the couch would make him dirty.

The analyst then pointed out to the group that one person completely absent in his self-reports was the governess, who must have played a considerable role in the patient's life because she had lived with the family.

A member of the group suggested that there was a primary fixation in this case around the dyadic relationship I. had with his mother. He not only regressed in an almost autistic way back to this symbiosis—with the analyst the only other person whom he tried to entrap into playing this role—but he regressed as well from a triadic or oedipal situation. This suggested that his behavior pattern was deeply determined, and the perverse aspect was in the intense pleasure in being nice to himself.

The analyst reported that, in the following session, he asked the analyst whether he should transfer to art school. In this period, he had again been failing to attend classes; he simply remained at home, sleeping or listening to music or making tea. He wanted the analyst to make the decision for him, which of course the analyst could not do. However, they discussed the alternatives of art school or a job, and the patient decided that he would take a job because he did not trust himself to attend the classes if he did transfer to art school. In this self-evaluation, the analyst felt he was being quite realistic. Another factor that entered into the decision was that a job would be easier for him to accept because it was not what his parents would value—both his mother and father wished him to continue with college. An ordinary job, such as a salesman in a store, would be looked down upon by his family.

I. had reported to the analyst that when he went home for a brief holiday, he had gotten a haircut. The acquiescence was significant because, for him, long hair was really a sign of masculinity, whereas short hair represented submission to the mother. He returned to his discussion of taking a job and raised many obstacles, including the problem of scheduling his analytic hour. The analyst told him that this was something that they would have to work out, since he could not choose his hours if he were working.

I. obtained a position as assistant in the restoration department of a museum. After an adjustment period during which the analyst had to rearrange his schedule, I. was given an appointment for after working hours. When the patient arrived, he reported that he felt weak, drained of energy, and thought it was cruel that he was expected to travel by public transportation to his job and be subjected to such an inhuman ordeal. He blamed his father, feeling that his father should give him enough money to support himself so that he would be able to do nothing.

Actually the father's position had been that I. must either

attend college or take a job to support himself. He had never threatened not to pay for analysis. I. was terribly lonely, and his silence was a plea for the analyst to talk, to make him feel alive. He noticed some flowers on the analyst's table and was curious to know who selected and arranged them, and questioned the analyst about his favorite flower.

On the way out, he commented, "I like your flower arrangement better than my mother's—she is so orderly and meticulous about it." The analyst reported that I. was reading two homosexual books and that he spoke of his envy of the authors, who found someone they could love. He felt that he was less interested in being loved than in finding someone he could love. The analyst felt that this was a defense and that actually he wished to be loved. For example, he loved one of his co-workers, but the young man did not return the feeling.

On the subject of being loved and loving, I. reported further that he told his mother that she had stopped loving him when she stopped doing what he wanted her to do. "She always told me what to do." It was after this comment that he reported the incident of the haircut and described his mother's happiness with his compliance. He then realized that the cosmetic attention that he paid to himself was very much like his mother's cosmetic attention to him. The realization had followed his mother's reaction to the haircut, and since it had occurred to him, he had felt extremely uncomfortable in her company.

He missed his next appointment, and during the one following he talked about his expectation that the analyst would allow him to miss an appointment, allow him to do what he wanted to do. The analyst replied, "Well, you feel that that would really be an expression of love." He responded, "I'm glad you got my message, when I talked about the flowers; and I like you better than my mother." He then asked immediately, "Why can't I stay and have dinner with you?" During this period, I. had overdrawn his bank account and his father had refused either to cover the overdraft or to co-sign a loan.

I. missed an appointment that had been made for his day off. When the analyst called him, he justified his absence by saying, "I went to the market." When he appeared for his next appointment, he was furious. He felt that the analyst was very angry with him.

with these interpretations, because he knew they were true. He recognized that his avoidance of his private thoughts was then acted out in resistance. In this acting-out, he did outside of the analysis what he was not willing to bring into the analysis; therefore the analyst still did not know much about his actual homosexual experiences or his fantasies.

The analyst then reported to the group two full sessions. I. had missed his first analytic hour after a vacation period. When the analyst called him, he said with great surprise, "Oh, I thought we start tomorrow." The analyst mentioned that he had thought that the time was perfectly clear, but that he would see him the next day.

When he arrived the next day, he was fifteen minutes late. Before he entered the analyst's room, he came toward the door, went back and looked into the waiting room, turned to the analyst, turned around again looking back into the waiting room, repeated this one more time, and finally came into the analyst's consulting room looking very bewildered. The analyst did not know what I. was looking for. The session began and after a brief reference to his absence of the day before, I. pushed the subject aside by saying, "Well, I didn't forget. I just didn't feel like coming and that was the simplest way to act when you called." He made no attempt to explain away the absence. Then he got a severe coughing fit which continued for some time until he asked, "Can I go and get a drink of water?" When he came back and lay down again, he told the analyst in a somewhat agitated voice, "There's a pair of rubbers in front of the door in the outside hall. Whose are they?" There was a silence, then he changed the subject and said, "I went to a party last Friday. I met a psychologist there who is a homosexual. Well, you know, it was a homosexual party. And this psychologist says he is a therapist. Now that's terrible. Don't you think so? I told the psychologist so and he claims that as long as you're well adjusted, it's all right." He then added, "I would just die if I found out that you were a homosexual." The analyst interpreted this as a response to the rubbers. They had given him a shock because there was no one in the waiting room, and he then felt that there must be a man hidden in the analyst's private quarters.

There was silence, then I. and the analyst talked about I.'s giving the analyst only bits of information about the homosexual party. I. responded, "Well, what am I supposed to tell you? After

The analyst had, in fact, not been angry, and he pointed out
that his absences really had nothing to do with being tired from
exertions of his job, since they could occur on a day when he s
until noon. He then realized that he was angry because the ana
would not yield permissively to his needs. He reacted by becom
extremely aggressive.

In a session that followed a cancellation by the analyst,
arrived saying that he felt an extreme urgency to come that day.
was not able to analyze the urgency, except to say that he need
money. He did not ask the analyst for money directly; the reque
was indirect. The analyst pointed out that he could not give hi
money; he could only give him insight. I., who now had an acu
realization of what analysis was, responded, "You are right; it's ni
that you put it this way." At another point, when he could not tal
or continue, he asked the analyst, "Now, you tell me why I shoul
talk," and then caught himself, saying "Don't answer it, I know it.
Clearly, despite all his resisting and playing with analysis and witl
the analyst, he very much respected the analyst's refusal to give ir
to his neurotic needs.

I. was now living with a great deal of insecurity. He had an
unresolved money problem, and although he had worked very well
on his job, arriving every day and working hard, the job would only
last a short time unless an opening could be found in another department. The reality situation was most uncertain. The analyst spent
great deal of time attempting to analyze I.'s absences, which I. de
fended simply by saying, "I don't feel like coming." The analy
pointed out four strands in this resistance: First were his deman
that the analyst understand his need to do what he wanted to
and that the analyst remain a benign friend who was always the
waiting; second was his aggressive feelings against his fath
expressed by forcing his father to waste money on sessions he
not attend; third was his wish to give the analyst pleasure
reading books, during a "free" session; fourth was the proc
involved when I. woke up and said to himself in the morning
will not see the doctor today," and was inundated by thoug
memories, and desires he wished to keep private. In effect,
analyst pointed out, I. attended sessions only when he was
defended, a pattern which the analyst described to him as, "W
you need to come least, then you are here." I. laughed and ag

the party I went home with a friend of mine who lives in the same neighborhood. He went his way and I went my way. What else do you want to know?" The analyst reminded I. of the letter he had written during the summer in which he said that he was constantly obsessed with homosexual thoughts, and I. replied, "Yes, that's true, but let's forget the letter. I am never going to talk about everything I did or do." He then noticed that the painting in the analyst's room had been changed. Again, silence. Then, "Did I tell you about my buying honey?" The analyst reminded him that he did. He said, "Well, I don't eat it any more, but I bought a lot. I now have a collection of twenty jars. And now I am buying soap, all different kinds of soap." The analyst asked him what his favorite soap was and I., showing embarrassment, said Yardley's Lavender. The analyst asked whether anyone in his family used it. He said, "Why do you ask that?" The analyst reminded him, "Don't you remember, the honey was served by your grandmother at breakfast when you were a little boy?" Again, he was extremely pleased by this constancy to him in the analyst's memory. The analyst allowed him this permissible pleasure. He then answered the questions. "Yes, my aunt." The analyst reported that this was an aunt whom he liked very much and whom he used to visit until the previous summer or fall, when she had showed her conventional side by criticizing him and giving him a pep talk about what he should do. Since that time he had not visited her.

The analyst pointed out to I. that as soon as he gave up an object—in this case, his aunt—he appropriated certain concrete features of that person and made them his own, like this collection of soap. I. and the analyst discussed the similarity between this behavior and the fact that I. continued to take good care of his skin, as his mother used to do.

I. then reported that when he had been home over the previous holiday, he had visited a lesbian bar for the second time. He commented, "These women are deformed." The analyst was unable to get at what he meant, because the term "deformed" has such a visually concrete aspect. He continued, "They were all in masculine dress. If they were dressed in dresses, you would think they are nice women." He felt at ease among them, unlike the way he usually felt in the company of women and girls. He merely looked at them and sat at the bar, where he talked with a truck driver. He said to the truck driver, "You know, I don't mind if these kind of women raise their voices at me. They are all right." The analyst was unable to elicit anything about his fantasies in this situation, but thought that the fact that he went back to the lesbian bar showed that he felt comfortable among women who have no interest in men.

He was twenty-five minutes late for the next session. He was silent, and the analyst allowed the silence to go on for twenty minutes. Then he asked, "Why can't you talk today?" I. responded, "I thought it would be a very good hour today, a very interesting one." The analyst replied, "You cut it short." I. then said, "I like to be late. Sometimes I like to be early. I had no feeling of not coming. I wanted to come very much." The analyst asked, "Is this being late something like the extras, as we once called them, for which you always ask?" I. replied, "Yes, very much so." About the silence, he said, "I often sit in my room and just think. It's very pleasant. It is just as pleasant now being quiet here, like sipping tea." The analyst replied, "It was a very good hour after all, both being silent; it is as pleasant as having tea together." I. said, "Yes, it is really very nice." The analyst reported that the patient was simply lying on the couch during the silence, not falling asleep, but playing with his hands as infants do. Only after enjoying the mutual silence was he able to put his feelings into words. The analyst commented that this session seemed to represent a very primitive identification of the nursling. He suggested that it may have been an expression, in the most literal sense, of a merging, in which his homosexuality was rerouted in a regressive, passive desire to merge. The analyst suggested further that the resistance, when he absented himself, might be a protection against a deep merging. He cited as evidence that when I. was absent, he thought of the analyst constantly and never had the slightest thought of terminating the analysis. No matter how far away he might be, he expected the analyst to think of him and he thought of the analyst, thus producing a merging in distance which was less dangerous than the threat of the actual merging when he was in the analyst's presence.

The analyst pointed out two things in past material that he found significant. The first was a fantasy concerning I.'s transvestism. I. reported that he was now spending a great deal of time fantasying that he was wearing a black velvet robe. "I want to be a vision," he said. The analyst asked him to describe the robe and he replied, "Well, like a toga; it means a gown, a long gown. It could also be white velvet, but I prefer black and with a white face." I. imagined himself entering a room and having all the people turn around and say, "There he is." In his fantasy, he always dressed that way, in order to be seen and noticed and to have a reputation. As he put it, "It's like being God—a distinct character, where one says, 'Oh, here he is, that black velvet vision.'" The analyst was unable to elicit any childhood memories that explained this specific fantasy. In reality, his dress and grooming were not exceptional, other than in his emphasis on cleanliness and taste. The analyst mentioned that at this point in the analysis, I. admitted that he had depressions. The fantasy seemed to be his method of rescuing himself from falling into a depression.

The analyst also reported a recent Monday session at which I. failed to appear. At his Tuesday session, he did not refer to his absence. When questioned, he said, "I just didn't measure the time right. I was cleaning the apartment and it got late. I was washing the kitchen floor." When the analyst reminded him of earlier statements that he could not do even those things he wanted to do, particularly if they coincided with something his mother wanted him to do or that the analyst wanted him to do, he said, "Well, as a matter of fact, when I started to wash the kitchen floor, I thought, if I start, it might get too late, and when I thought that this is what my mother would want me to do—clean up—I cleaned up and it was six o'clock." His appointment was for six o'clock, and it would have taken him half an hour to get to the office.

The analyst summed up his presentation by pointing out that he was handicapped because he did not know the details of his patient's sexual behavior, autoerotic behavior, or behavior with homosexual partners. He had to gain his insight into the patient from the bits and pieces he brought up associatively and in disconnected form, and most particularly in his transference behavior.

The analyst pointed out that the transference behavior indicated that the dynamics operated in stages which could not be lumped together under one denominator. On the earliest level, the patient had a need to establish a oneness with a lover, a merging; if he were prevented from reaching this, he was faced with the danger of an anaclitic depression. The patient had developed all kinds of maneuvers to protect himself against this depression. On another level, the analyst felt, the patient used a homosexual act as protection against a depressed affect, but this was a later developmental stage. It was understandable only if viewed in the perspective of its precursor, the oneness between child and mother, which later was transposed on the gender level.

As the father entered the scene more strongly, the patient easily obtained gratification from merging with an object of the same gender because the merging was based on primary narcissism. The question then might be: Why was the perverse or homosexual solution never transcended? The analyst felt that another element entered into the answer—the patient's need for concrete objects to give him a good feeling. His need could be satisfied, for example, by buying the honey and soap that substituted for object relations with his grandmother and his aunt, or by impulsively stealing material objects. The patient really had no feeling that there was anything wrong with stealing, and was not interested in why he stole or why he bought such things as the honey and the soap. The material objects were an end in themselves. In the same way, his attachment to analysis was an attachment to the analyst and the possible merging gratification the analysis represented.

The analyst pointed out that the defectiveness of the superego had a long history. The patient had a quasi-superego, which was merely a concrete identification with his mother. An interpretation, even though he recognized it as accurate, had no cogency. He simply experienced a direct gratification in that the analyst understood something about him, which was an end in itself. In this sense, interpretation represented a merging, but it did not stimulate development or insight.

The analyst ruled out the possibility of an impulse disorder, because the patient's every action was a concrete inner drama filled with enormous fantasies. He cited the last session he described, when I. explained why he had missed his previous hour. In his decision to wash the kitchen floor and thereby miss the appointment—a consequence he had anticipated—there was a complete inner drama which the patient never disclosed. It was, however, an involved psychic conflict: "Should I listen to mother or should I listen to father?" When he decided to listen to his mother, that choice permitted him to avoid the father, whom the analyst represented on that day.

The patient had a quality of merely floating through experience; of ambivalence; of never being completely capable of carrying anything through, either in his academic work or in his object relations. This quality was also evident in his analysis. He was impelled by a variety of drives but appeared to be caught between the need for gratification and the defenses against it. Since all of his actions and nonactions had a psychic content, it was not appropriate to describe his behavior as an impulse disorder; it appeared, rather, to be a neurotic disturbance characterized by an elaboration of fantasy and inhibitions. There was also a strong theme of passivity underlying his behavior—a libidinization of passivity in a very fundamental sense. This factor would seem to require an intensive exploration of his relationship with the mother. His virtual isolation also underscored the dyadic, passive orientation in which he assumed the role of the compulsive, perfectionist mother.

The patient was completely enmeshed in a concreteness of affect and response. He became "real" through concrete objects which he gathered about him. His excessive concern with dress had a narcissistic element, and his constant fantasy about a costume played a complementary exhibitionist role. The fantasies also provided an escape from depression.

The patient had a special position with regard to his instinctual needs; he had to have what he wanted and brooked no frustration. This impulsivity was evident in his responses to the lack of control and frustration attendant on the analysis. As with similar cases considered by the group, the patient was caught up in needs that could be gratified in minor but extremely concrete ways, and he avoided the abstract character of words which he could not use for problem solving or even for partial gratification. In contrast, the gratification provided by the patient's homosexual fantasies appeared to be substantially greater than any real action could provide.

In general, the vicissitudes in the transference reflected a recapitulation of the patient's history of object relations. He could never find comfort since he could not completely tolerate the analyst in any of his roles: mother, father, the sausage or spike of his early dream. Yet the substitution of narcissistic gratification for any gratification provided by the analyst was also unsatisfactory, because it imposed on him an intolerable loneliness.

The transference also indicated a number of other dynamic patterns: the patient wished, through "forcing" the analyst to inject personal comments, to be verbally penetrated and to be nurtured. The analyst's silence also represented a vaginalike entrapment; the interaction provided the certainty of the analyst's phallus. At the same time, the patient interpreted the analyst's interest as a homosexual approach from which he must flee. Members of the group speculated that the patient had experienced what he perceived as a series of desertions—by the mother, the father, and the counsellor —which interfered with his ability to develop sound object relations and to tolerate frustrations. All action was object oriented, as exemplified in his statement that when he knew his mother wanted him to do something that he also wanted to do, he was embarrassed. This suggested a libidinized imitation or identification that attached to any activity; he defended against this closeness (loss of identity) by removing himself from the act.

The aggression-revenge component of forthright homosexual behavior generated ambiguity and fear. It does not seem to be a guilt or superego mechanism; it was a projective id mechanism that made the acting-out of the perversion dangerous. The patient was torn between the aggressive impulse and the attendant fear.

The analyst viewed the patient's resistance, in the form of personal questions about the analyst and anger when the questions were not answered, as a homosexual defense; the patient wished to be "penetrated" by the analyst's verbal responses to his questions. Similarly, talking about sex was equivalent to a sexual relation with the analyst. His response to the subject of sex was so concrete and literal that he avoided it because it played such a vital role in the libidinization of his relationship to the analyst. These characteristics —the need for concrete and actual experience, the concomitant inhibition of action, the relative weakness of the superego, and the unresponsiveness to words—suggested a fixation at an early preoedipal, dyadic stage of development.

CASE VI

This twenty-five-year-old man, K. L., entered analysis with the presenting psychiatrist, expressing a vague complaint of homosexuality and "some business with horses." It became apparent that overt homosexuality was not his problem; rather, he was frightened by impulses toward it.

The "business with horses" turned out to be a compulsive desire to ride horses, preferably stallions, and to experience an ejaculation (which the patient called "an emission") as he leaned forward along the horse's neck. Frequently, he attempted to force the horse down on its knees so that the neck was stretched out toward the ground.

The patient was an adopted child. His father had been the fifth child, and only son, in a family of eight children. Before the arrival of his younger sisters, he was the long-desired boy and was adored by his mother. However, after the arrival of his two younger sisters, he no longer received the same kind of mothering. The analyst had the impression that, in this overwhelmingly feminine milieu, the patient's father had little opportunity to establish a masculine identity.

The adoptive father's family was by no means wealthy, and five of his sisters worked. However, his mother was extremely ambitious for him and he was sent to college—the only member of his family to receive a higher education. For a time he worked to help pay his way, and played football well, but accomplished little scholastically. He became an athletic star and received an athletic scholarship. Later, after serving in the navy, he wanted to continue his athletic career, but his mother ordered him to marry a rich girl and go into business. Although he was not at all interested in girls, he acceded to his mother's wishes and married an heiress, four or five years older than he. Subsequently, in revenge and resentment against his own compliance, he cut off all contact with his sisters and expressed a passionate hatred for his mother.

K.'s maternal grandfather was described as a typical Prussian, a strong, tall man, "cruel and nasty" or "fierce and mighty." His wife died when the boy's mother was only four years old, leaving two older sons as well as the daughter. A few years later, K.'s grandfather remarried.

After her mother's death, the patient's mother had been sent to live with her older brother and was happy in the care of her sister-in-law. After her father's remarriage, she was brought back to his home but was never happy with her stepmother.

Although the patient's mother was raised as an Episcopalian, she was educated in a convent. Perhaps, she considered becoming a nun to escape a developing depressive psychosis; her sister-in-law influenced her to choose marriage, instead. The analyst felt that she undoubtedly suffered from a lack of mothering, but she believed that she had a father-complex, and married a man who superficially resembled her father.

Her husband, K.'s adoptive father, did not give her much tenderness. She had frequent crying spells and since she could not become pregnant, she tried to resist depression by adopting K.

From his earliest years, K. was raised by nurses. The last one in his life, "Nanny," remained with the family throughout his childhood, and he was extremely close to her. In contrast, his mother was very distant. She seemed to remember his existence only when she gave parties, at which time she presented him to her guests as a curio.

Toilet training began when K. was two years old. Apparently, his nurse began his training in a park zoo, within sight of the horses. His family claimed that he was toilet trained in two weeks, but K. himself said that he was enuretic until he was six years old.

His father's behavior with him was teasing. His father, who wanted the child to become an extension of himself, began training him early for the athletic career he himself had had to terminate. He let K. ride piggyback; he threw him up in the air and caught him; in the morning, while he was lying on his bed, he allowed him to crawl over him, and they "roughhoused."

The analyst thought that the father might have been aware of an erection and of pederastic impulses because, according to the patient, he often pushed his son away suddenly and fled into a cold shower.

Sometimes, he took his son with him into the bathroom. K. was startled when he saw the gush and heard the loud splashing in the toilet bowl as his father urinated. In spite of his adopted mother's struggle against depression, she developed an acute psychotic disorder and was hospitalized when K. was only two and a half years old. He and his nurse then went to stay with his uncle and aunt, who lived nearby in the same East Coast city. They were delighted to have a child in the house and apparently spoiled him. K. remembered those days with nostalgia. Every Christmas thereafter he was invited to his aunt's home to share their Christmas tree and receive his gifts. Sometimes he stole ornaments from the tree.

When K.'s mother returned home, the family moved from the city to a roomy suburban home with grounds. K.'s father bought him a pony as a pet. When the boy recoiled from the horse, his father was disappointed and called him a "sissy." This incident seemed to be the first truly traumatic event in the patient's life.

When K. was four, he was sent to kindergarten. At five, he was hospitalized with scarlet fever. When his mother visited him, she told him that he was adopted and, to her surprise, he reacted with pleasure. The analyst felt the child's reaction derived from his feelings about his mother's coldness and his close attachment to his nurse. When the boy went home, he found that his parents had a younger child, who was presented to him as his sister. During his hospitalization, his father had given away the pony K. had seemed to fear; the child was very distressed and felt that his sister had taken its place.

There were multiple rejections in the patient's life at this time: his beloved nurse had little time left for him because she was caring for his sister; his father was increasingly reluctant to engage in "horseplay" with him. In an attempt to make contact, K. provoked and bullied his playmates. Once, in an argument with a cousin of whom he was jealous because his father seemed to prefer him, the patient ordered the cousin, in a rather "king of the hill" fashion, to get off his property. His cousin retaliated by taunting him about being an adopted child, saying that his father was not really his father. Apparently K. had not fully understood his mother's earlier statement, because this taunt threw him into a panic. He ran to his mother to ask her about his origin and that of his sister. She confirmed that he was not a natural son, but consoled him by telling him that he was a child of God, that he came from The Cradle, and that when he grew up he could, if he wished, even marry his sister.

The pony his father had given away was never replaced by another pet. However, K.'s sister was given kittens and K. joined her in playing with them. The patient reported that his father always killed the kittens when they matured, usually by thrusting a pen knife through the cat's ear into the brain, often in the presence of the children.

When K. was of school age, he was enrolled in an exclusive private school in a nearby city, to which he commuted. When he learned to read, his favorite book was one of *The Wizard of Oz* series, which his nurse had often read to him. The book contained a character called Mombie, a witch who turned Princess Ozma, the rightful ruler of Oz, into a boy

In these early years, the child had close contact with his mother only when he had nightmares. She consoled him by taking him into her bed.

Between the ages of six and eight, he spent his summers away at camp. His parents visited him there only once, and in adult life he recalled that he had been unable to sleep that night, knowing that his parents were in the nearby town.

His parents envisaged conflicting roles for him. His mother taught him to play the piano; his father, at the same time, was training him for an athletic career.

When K. was twelve, he finally rebutted his father's early accusation that he was a sissy by learning to ride a horse. To his surprise, he had an ejaculation during the ride. He was frightened and told his mother about it, but she reacted only with embarrassment. He then told his father, who advised him to take a cold shower, warned about the perils of masturbation, and made some comments about girls that the patient failed to understand.

For a while, K. was able to go horseback riding without having this sexual response; then it happened again. This time, when he told his father, the father "got mad," according to the patient's report.

Although the patient claimed that his father disliked women and that he had never seen him kiss his mother, he reported that he had seen him kiss his little sister and had felt furiously jealous.

The analyst felt that the horseback riding was secondary to the search for the pony his father had given away; grief over the loss of the pony was somehow equated with his hatred of his sister.

By this time, the patient had begun teasing and mistreating his sister. He seemed to assume that because he was adopted, no one had the right to forbid him to do anything. His behavior was unmanageable; he obeyed only his beloved aunt and nurse. Ostensibly on the grounds of the boy's need for discipline, his father sent him to a military school. The analyst felt, however, that the father made this choice because he was uncertain about his son's masculinity.

At eighteen, the patient entered an eastern Ivy League college, where he majored in music. He then spent two years in the army, much of it in Germany, England, and Texas. In England, he attended a three-month course at a London college of music. After two years in the army, he returned to college.

The perversion involving horses first developed when the patient was twelve and persisted thereafter. The analyst felt the perversion protected him from acting out his homosexual impulses, but did not relieve his anxiety about them.

At college, while studying for his bachelor's degree, he became increasingly confused. He wrote to his mother, who was then in analysis with a woman analyst in the city in which the family lived. She advised him to seek treatment and referred him to a woman psychoanalyst in his college town. His mother offered to pay for the analysis, since his father was a Christian Scientist and opposed all physicians, particularly psychiatrists.

The patient took his mother's advice and entered analysis. However, he was reticent about his daydreams and his perverse behavior, and refused to talk about his religious fantasies because he felt that to mention these would be sacrilegious. Early in treatment, he remarked to the analyst that he was sure he would be allowed to graduate from college without taking his examinations. The suggestion made her laugh, and the patient reported, "That scared me to death"; he thought she was a witch. He told the analyst that his nurse was his real mother, but she pointed out that this was impossible because his nurse was too old to have been his mother.

Early in the course of treatment, this first analyst took a long holiday weekend. The patient masturbated that weekend for the first time in his life. K. was rooming with a young seminary student to whom he was homosexually attracted. Out of extreme guilt about these feelings, he applied for another roommate. These events all occurred during the analyst's absence. Remembering his mother's frequent threat to convert to Catholicism, the patient went to an early Catholic Mass. He began talking excitedly about girls, which he had never done before. K. then went to the school infirmary to consult the psychologist about his analyst's credentials. He asked for an allergy test, because he didn't want to eat red meat. Then he poured out all of his fantasies: that he was originally a girl who had been turned into a boy; that being a Catholic meant that he could not eat meat.

Apparently his behavior alarmed the psychologist, who immediately had the patient hospitalized. He remained in the hospital for six weeks, during which his analyst visited him daily. For the first three weeks, he was in bed, then became an outpatient in order to take his examinations

After the school year was over, K. returned to his home. His mother took him to see her analyst, who had seen him twice before and had advised him to enter psychoanalytic treatment. She referred K. to the presenting analyst.

Early in the course of this second analysis, K. reported his perverse behavior and other important material without any resistance. He formed an immediate transference, which on the surface seemed to be a negative one, but which the analyst soon realized was an erotized transference. The patient's reports of behavior which endangered him were intended to elicit an angry response: a repetition of the teasing behavior pattern of the patient's childhood. For example, he reported to the analyst:

> After school I went to the stables. It was dark. I stroked a horse and began to masturbate it, but it did not get an erection. It was castrated. So I went to the next horse, which was also castrated. I wanted the horse to kneel down so that I could get on top of it. One horse got down, but I didn't ejaculate. Then I went home and masturbated, with the fantasy that I was masturbating my father's penis . . . The Easter weekend bothered me. I sang in the choir on Good Friday, but I didn't like the accompaniment to the last words of Christ on the Cross, it was too pompous. . . . I had dinner with my aunt. I got upset about it and felt uneasy. . . . You asked me why I never thought of buying a horse? Why then should I have the analysis? (He had mentioned that he could buy a horse for only $200.)

In the ninth hour he reported his first dream.

> I was outside, on the campus, in the spring. There were trees and flowers around me. Then suddenly I was in a garage, looking for horses. All the horses were out. I asked the mechanic and he said, "You can wash these horses," as if they were cars or trucks. Then I was looking for Bob (his college roommate). Then I was in some other place. I seemed to sneak up behind a fellow as if I was going to put my penis in his rectum. It wasn't Bob, it was one of the fellows at the company.

> It was Spring when I got out of the hospital last year. I was not supposed to see Bob, it was forbidden. Bob was religious. He went into the ministry. I thought he would help and I told him my feelings for him and for the horses and began to cry. He went out of the room. He knew that I saw a psychiatrist and I think he was jealous because I turned to someone else. I told her once that she was a lesbian and a Communist. She wanted me to tell her the things I did, but I could never overcome the resistance, especially about the religious experience because she would not understand it. (This last was a reference to the fact that the woman psychoanalyst was Jewish.)

The patient's father had gotten him a job in the company in which he was employed.

> At the company my job is adding up figures, paper work. I try

to get through it fast so that I can look for horses. I am also doing choral work now and things are mixed up. Evidently there are still feelings about you. I suppose that I call you a Communist. (He then referred back to his college friend Bob, in whose arms he wants to die when they are both old. He feels that his work in the church will keep him with Bob, and the analyst interprets this as a wish for fusion.) I looked in the phone book for addresses of stables; they directed me to various places and finally I came to a place where there was a garage and no stables any more. I read Sherwood Anderson's book *Men and Horses,* and it got me sexually excited. So does any magazine on the Wild West. There is a story of a man jumping on the neck of a terrified horse. I thought I shouldn't read it, but I looked through the whole magazine to find the continuation. In regard to the man I was coming up on in the dream, I don't know whether he had any clothes on. I always feel very self-conscious and look around for well-built fellows, somebody like Bob. When I saw the lady analyst, it was harder and harder to have anything to do with Bob. It is love and fear. When I finally was lying in bed and masturbated I thought I was released and then thought I would change sexually and when I see him again I will change back. This is the situation with father. I am afraid to show my feelings for him, but maybe it was the other way around. My reaction to meeting Bob's brother was guilt. I had done nothing for him while he was here. Bob and I were in prep school together. He was kicked out of school for misbehavior, but his father was powerful. I was very impressed by the whole family, visited them and was kind of agog the whole time, as if I were his bride.

In a later hour, the patient reported a wet dream in which he set fire to a stable and savored the agonized shrieking of the horses.

In the nineteenth hour, he reported a wet dream in which he pulled on a horse's neck; the horse lifted him up, pulled back, and threw him over its head into the air. This was exactly what his father had done in their roughhousing.

Earlier, the patient had told the analyst that he liked to get on a horse and, while having an ejaculation, bite its neck. In a more bizarre and more exciting activity (which the analyst felt was probably fantasy), he would bind the horse's hoofs and force it onto its

Late in the first year of the analysis, the patient reported a back, so that its penis pointed upward. His greatest wish-fulfillment fantasy was to mount a stallion while it was mounting a mare.

dream about a graduation party at his college, from which he had not in fact graduated. As he reported the dream, it occurred to him that he wanted to have an ejaculation simultaneously with Bob. However, he never acted out his homosexuality.

In the second year of analysis, the patient began dating a girl of whom his father disapproved, although his mother liked her. The patient told his girl friend that she would receive a threatening letter from his father. He would visit horses before he went to see the girl. He also masturbated, short of ejaculation, in order *to retain enough power to control her.*

He reported a dream in which his entire family and all their friends were gathered together. His mother was mad at his father. His father went to the toilet and the boy went with him. His father leaned over the urinal, vomiting, urinating, and defecating simultaneously. "I said," reported the patient, " 'Oh, you will have to go home.' Dad said, 'No,' took a rag, and wiped his behind and his mouth. I was in a corner and he threw the rag at me, but I was glad. I followed him outside and in the presence of all the people squeezed the rag over him."

His sister, who had reached twenty-two, had taken a job as a waitress. His father gave her twenty-two dollars for her birthday but at the same time threatened to disown her for taking such a menial job.

"In my family," the patient complained, "everyone hates everyone."

In the next hour he reported a dream in which he was kept prisoner in an old frame house by the ringleader of a gangster family because he had committed a murder. The corpse was found on the outside porch. There was money involved

He told the analyst he wanted to work as organist in the church, so that he would be free to marry his girl. She had actively encouraged his involvement in church work.

Another girl he met at church helped him find an apartment of his own. She was rich and adored her brother, in whom the patient saw another Bob, so that he could identify with her. He felt comfortable with her because she was "incapable of affection," unlike his girl friend, who, he felt, was almost holding him "on a string." Both girls were older than he.

He told the analyst that, in order to avoid a commitment to

either girl, he was going to quit his job and marry his sister. The analyst admitted that this would not be incest, but warned him that he would find it difficult to earn a living by composing music. Nevertheless, the patient announced his decision to his boss. A few days later, in tears, he admitted that he had made a stupid mistake. His boss allowed him to return to his job, but he continued to make a nuisance of himself (much as he had as a child).

In the third year of the analysis, the patient had a dream in which he pulled an old man out of a well which was inside a house, and then that men were digging a well in the neighbor's house. The analyst interpreted the dream as a primal-scene fantasy (digging a well). He felt that pulling the old man out of the well represented pulling the penis out of a horse's prepuce, or pulling the father out of the mother's vagina so that she would not get pregnant.

In another dream, the analyst was a blacksmith hammering nails into a horse's hoof. This was so clearly an erotized transference dream that the analyst decided to restrain his therapeutic ambition, and refused to react to the patient's horse stories and the avalanche of manure the patient was offering him. The patient responded to this withdrawal with sullen silence and threats to stop the analysis. He was cooperative in one respect: he had accepted the analyst's statement that in order to escape from his perversion, he had to date. He had already begun going out with another girl who was determined enough not to become discouraged by the patient.

When the patient's father's firm was taken over by a larger company, the patient's father retained his job but knew that there was no longer any opportunity for advancement. In his disappointment, he wanted to groom K. to become an executive. However, the patient refused to become a businessman; he still wanted to become a celebrated composer.

One day the father appeared in the analyst's office, furious because he had been kept waiting. In a typically paranoid manner, he accused the analyst of alienating his wife and his son from him, complained about the money the treatment was costing, and threatened to create a scandal. He had learned about the analysis accidentally. The analyst could calm him only by mentioning that he was a consultant for a Veterans Administration Hospital.

Shortly thereafter, both parents underwent physical examinations at well-known medical clinics. A letter to the patient's mother arrived during her absence. K. read it and learned that his father was suffering from metastatic malignancy. He began looking forward to the imminent deaths of both his adoptive parents, the money he would inherit, and the house he planned to buy and use as a boys' music school in which he would teach composition.

Without his father's authorization, the patient notified his father's company of his illness, probably hoping he would inherit his father's job. Shortly thereafter, his father committed suicide.

In the analytic hour following the suicide, the patient, crying, accused himself of missing every opportunity to tell his father that he loved him. Several days thereafter, however, he focussed again on his hopes for an inheritance.

The conflict between a career in business and one in music was reinforced when his company offered to send him to a special training course. His girl friend, fearful of losing him, pressed for some commitment, but the analyst advised him against getting married without having had any heterosexual experience. The patient tried to delay this anxiety-producing task by citing the girl's traditional inhibition against premarital intercourse. After some months, they became formally engaged, but still had not had sexual relations. Finally, one evening they faced each other nude. K. was unable to have an erection then, but the next attempt was successful, and two months later they were married.

A month after his wedding, he quit his job. He planned to return to school and qualify as a music teacher, relying upon a part-time job and his wife's salary to support them. He continued in analysis for another year and then terminated, supposedly because his wife wanted to have a baby and, without her income, they would be unable to afford treatment. He finally did accept an opportunity for a rewarding career in business, though he retained an avocational interest in music. The last dream the patient reported was a postcoital dream, in which everyone was piling on each other, as in a football game.

The analyst believed that the hippophilic perversion was first triggered by the patient's being called a sissy by his adoptive father. The analyst suggested that, "As soon as the patient reached puberty, he felt compelled to disprove his father's accusation, but riding a horse was no longer merely a sport. Because of his more astute understanding of the meaning of the word "sissy," horseback riding became erotized. After the additional shock of learning of his adoption, the game with the horse had to subserve the acting-out of all his fantasies and needs resulting from his lack of identity. The perversion thus became overdetermined."

The analyst suggested further that, having been deprived by his cousin of the security he obtained from his "king of the hill" game, he had to regain control. Control implied power, and the horse sustained his quest for power.

Whenever the patient felt he was losing power, he returned to the horse for replenishment. When masturbation made him feel emasculated, he could restore his sexual power by touching the horse's phallus.

The father's roughhousing, which overstimulated the patient without permitting him any outlet, was reenacted in the patient's perversion. The adoption had deprived him of his real mother; he felt cheated and was able to rationalize his tendency to parasitize his adoptive parents.

The sadistic element in the perversion was aroused by the father's roughhousing and was reinforced by his observation of his his father's sadism in killing the cats.

The horse was not the patient's only sexual outlet. He had once described vividly the "spastic convulsions" of a kitten he had hurled to the floor. This incident, the analyst suggested, was indicative not only of the patient's sadism but also of his equation of the agonies of death with orgasm. In the same manner, he equated a fit of rage or madness with sexual orgasm.

The patient's fluid ego boundaries indicated that he was a horse himself, a centaur, and probably the lost pony as well.

Another member of the group asked: "Why was he unable to drop the perversion? Why couldn't he be freed of the irrational tendencies by genetic interpretations, with the assistance of the transference motivation?" Another member referred to the eidetic, specifically vivid quality of the symbolic process which, from childhood, made the visual image of the horse so important to the patient.

The analyst believed that the persistence of the perversion was based less on the eidetic capacity of the symbol than on a conditioned reflex. He pointed out that the Gestalt of the horse was perceived prior to the incident with the pony; it was established during early toilet training which began in a park near the stables. It thus became something like the gastrocolic reflex. The toilet training itself was overstimulating because it was started prematurely. Then the adoptive father, ashamed of his inability to have a child, overstimulated his son to make him an extension of himself, and to deny the adoption. After the pony had been introduced, elimination, the father, and the horse were fused into one synergic instinctual stimulus.

Under the influence of the transference, the patient was able to stay away from horses for some time, but the analyst felt that this restraint was possible only because the patient had merged him into a horse-father-analyst image.

NOTES ON
THE STUDY GROUP

Participants:

MORTIMER OSTOW, M.D., was Chairman of
the study group on sexual deviation. He was
at the same time President of the Psychoanalytic Research Development Fund and
also Chairman of its study group dealing
with a psychoanalytic investigation of psychiatric drug therapy. He is currently Vice-
President of the Fund and has initiated its
new study on the future of psychoanalysis.
Dr. Ostow is also Edward T. Sandrow Visiting Professor of Pastoral Psychiatry at The
Jewish Theological Seminary and Director
of its Morris J. Bernstein Center for Pastoral
Counseling. He has written on many subjects
in the fields of neurology, psychiatry, and
psychoanalysis. His books include *Drugs in
Psychoanalysis and Psychotherapy* and *The
Psychology of Melancholy.*

PETER BLOS, Ph.D., was trained as a
biologist in Vienna. His early professional
life was concerned with education and when
he became an analyst, he focused on the
problems of adolescence. In addition to his

181

many papers on the subject, he has written three books. He is a member of the faculty of The New York Psychoanalytic Institute and of The Columbia University Psychoanalytic Clinic for Training and Research.

SIDNEY FURST, M.D., is Professional Director of the Psychoanalytic Research and Development Fund and Chairman of its current study group on aggression. He was the editor of the first volume published by the Fund, *Psychic Trauma*. Dr. Furst is a member of the faculty of The New York Psychoanalytic Institute, of the Department of Psychiatry of The College of Physicians and Surgeons of Columbia University, and of the Department of Pastoral Psychiatry of The Jewish Theological Seminary. He is currently Chairman of the Committee on Psychiatry and Religion of The Group for the Advancement of Psychiatry.

GEORGE GERO, Ph.D., M.D., is a member of the faculty of The New York Psychoanalytic Institute and teaches in the Department of Psychiatry at The Albert Einstein College of Medicine. He has published widely on psychoanalytic subjects.

MARK KANZER, M.D., is Clinical Professor of Psychiatry at The State University of New York (Downstate) and a member of the faculty of The Division of Psychoanalytic Education at Downstate, having been its Director. He is a member of the editorial board of The International Journal of Psychoanalytic Psychiatry. Dr. Kanzer has written on many subjects in the field of clinical psychoanalysis, psychoanalytic theory and history.

DANIEL SILVERMAN, M.D., has conducted successful careers simultaneously in neurology and psychoanalysis. He was President of The Philadelphia Association for Psychoanalysis, of The Philadelphia Neurologic Society, and of The American Electroencephalographic Society, as well as Editor of the Bulletin of The Philadelphia Association for Psychoanalysis. His bibliography includes almost 100 papers, mostly on psychoanalysis and electroencephalography. Dr. Silverman withdrew from this project in 1967 because of ill health and died in 1971.

RICHARD S. STERBA, M.D., a practicing psychoanalyst in the Detroit area, is Professor Emeritus of Clinical Psychiatry at Wayne State University in Detroit. He has been interested in the change in culture of the Western world especially during the five decades of his psychoanalytic practice. He considers the key changes to be liberation from restrictions of sexual gratification, change in relation to parental and other authorities, and emotional disorientation. These changes, he finds, give rise to technical problems in psychoanalytic therapy.

ARTHUR S. VALENSTEIN, M.D., is President of the Boston Psychoanalytic Society and Institute and has been an instructor and training analyst at the Institute since 1957. Since 1971 he has been a Vice-President of the International Psychoanalytic Society. At Harvard Medical School he serves as Associate Clinical Professor of Psychiatry. He has been interested in psychoanalytic education, in observation and research into early development, including normative and deviate aspects, with a special interest in interrelated aspects of theories of affect and object relations; and the nature and theory of psychoanalysis as a "curative" process.

Guests:

JACOB A. ARLOW, M.D., is Clinical Professor of Psychiatry at The State University of New York and a member of the faculty of The New York Psychoanalytic Institute and of The Division of Psychoanalytic Education, Downstate. He is the author of many important contributions on psychoanalytic theory and practice.

EARL A. LOOMIS, JR., M.D., is Psychiatric Director of Blueberry Treatment Center for schizophrenic children in Brooklyn. He served as Professor of Psychiatry and Religion at Union Theological Seminary from 1956 to 1963. At the same time he was Attending Psychiatrist and Chief of Child Psychiatry at Saint Luke's Hospital in New York City.

ERNEST A. RAPPAPORT, M.D., commenced his medical career in Vienna in the late 1920s. His experiences as an inmate of the concentration camp at Buchenwald gave him the opportunity to make observations on situations of extreme psychic stress, subsequently published when he came to the United States. He is Clinical Professor of Psychiatry at Chicago Medical School and Senior Attending Psychiatrist at Michael Reese and Mount Sinai hospitals in Chicago. His other publications deal with subjects in clinical psychoanalysis, and psychological aspects of vision.

INDEX

Rebirth experience, perverse act as, 27-28, 32-33
Regression, 41-42, 48-50
Reich, Wilhelm, 55
Rejection of perverse tendency, 62
Replication of childhood event, 42, 44
Resistance in analysis, 56-57
Resumption of perverse behavior in analyst's absence, 59
Ritual action, 33, 44, 51
Role playing, 44, 57

Sadism, 31, 32, 61
Sadomasochism, 19-21, 61
Seductiveness in mother, 13-14, 16
Self-image, 41, 57; of male homosexual, 28-29, 30
Sexual: and aggressive impulses, fusion of, 19-20, 42; deviation (*see* Perversion); gratification, 33, 42, 62; inadequacy, sense of, 29-30, 41; object (*see* Object of sexual instinct)
Shame, 53
Solitary acts of perversion, 2-3, 5
Superego, 26, 27, 33, 48-53
Symptom formation and perversion distinguished, 25-27

Transference, 49, 55-56, 58-60
Treatment of perversion, 54-62

Visual sensitivity, 8, 30, 36-39, 55

Withdrawal as defense against anxiety, 27-28
Women, 18-19, 33-35